Routledge Revivals

Ceylon

Ceylon

Lord Holden

First published in 1939 by George Allen & Unwin Ltd.

This edition first published in 2018 by Routledge
2 Park Square, Milton Park, Abingdon, Oxon, OX14 4RN
and by Routledge
711 Third Avenue, New York, NY 10017

Routledge is an imprint of the Taylor & Francis Group, an informa business

© 1939 by Taylor & Francis

All rights reserved. No part of this book may be reprinted or reproduced or utilised in any form or by any electronic, mechanical, or other means, now known or hereafter invented, including photocopying and recording, or in any information storage or retrieval system, without permission in writing from the publishers.

Publisher's Note
The publisher has gone to great lengths to ensure the quality of this reprint but points out that some imperfections in the original copies may be apparent.

Disclaimer
The publisher has made every effort to trace copyright holders and welcomes correspondence from those they have been unable to contact.

A Library of Congress record exists under ISBN: 39033078

ISBN 13: 978-1-138-60506-0 (hbk)
ISBN 13: 978-1-138-60507-7 (pbk)
ISBN 13: 978-0-429-46219-1 (ebk)

by Lord Holden

FOUR GENERATIONS OF OUR
ROYAL FAMILY

ELEGANT MODES IN THE
NINETEENTH CENTURY

UNCLE LEOPOLD
A LIFE OF THE FIRST KING OF THE BELGIANS

With Ralph Dutton
ENGLISH HOUSES OPEN TO
THE PUBLIC
(Second Edition)

FRENCH CHÂTEAUX OPEN
TO THE PUBLIC

CEYLON

by
LORD HOLDEN

London
GEORGE ALLEN & UNWIN LTD

FIRST PUBLISHED IN 1939

All rights reserved

PREFACE

✣

I am greatly indebted to Mr. A. H. Longhurst, head of the Archaeological Survey of Ceylon, for his permission to publish the photographs of the Kantaka Cetiya, the Anuradhapura "Moonstone," the Thuparama and Lankatilaka at Polonnaruwa and of Sigiriya. I am also grateful to Mr. Aloysius Perera for allowing me to reproduce his photographs of the leopard and of the tank in the jungle. The remaining photographs were taken by myself.

HOLDEN

December, 1938

CONTENTS

✷

	PAGE
PREFACE	5

CHAPTER *Part One*

1. INTRODUCTION TO CEYLON AND THE CEYLONESE — 13
2. THE REST-HOUSE — 30
3. THE LORD BUDDHA — 52
4. *a.* THE MAHAWAMSA, OR THE GREATER DYNASTY — 64
   b. THE SULAWAMSA, OR THE LESSER DYNASTY — 83
5. THE LOST CITIES — 107
   a. The Dagoba — 107
   b. Tissamaharama — 109
   c. Mihintale — 111
   d. Anuradhapura — 116
   e. Polonnaruwa — 134
   f. Yapahuwa — 145
6. SIGIRIYA, OR THE LION ROCK — 148
7. SOME BUDDHIST TEMPLES — 160
   a. The Dalada Maligawa, or Temple of the Tooth, and the Nata Dewala, the Maha Dewala, the Malwatta, and the Degaldoruwa temples at Kandy — 160
   b. Dambulla — 169
   c. Isurumuniya — 172
   d. Aluvihare — 175
   e. Gedi-Gé — 176
   f. Aukana Vihara — 177
8. THE JUNGLE — 180

Ceylon

Part Two

PLEASANT JOURNEYS

	PAGE
A—*Colombo. Thence to Mount Lavinia, Kalutara, Galle, Matara, Tangalla, Hambantota, Wellawaya, Pottuvil, Batticaloa, Kalkuda, and Trincomalee*	213
B—*Trincomalee to Horawapotana, Vavuniya, Mankulam, Mullaittivu, and Jaffna: returning via Mankulam, Vavuniya, and Madawachchiya to Mannar; Madawachchiya to Anuradhapura, Mihintale, and Trincomalee*	243
C—*Trincomalee to Kantalai, Kekirawa, Dambulla, Nalanda, Matale, and Kandy. The three routes from Kandy to Colombo:*	257
(1) *Via Kurunegala and Negombo, one hundred miles.*	
(2) *Via Ginigathena Gap and Avisawella, ninety-five miles.*	
(3) *Via Kegalla and Veyangoda, seventy-two miles.*	
D—*Colombo to Negombo, Chilaw, Kalpitiya, Puttalam, Anuradhapura, and Kekirawa*	282
E—*Kandy to Nuwara Eliya by two routes:*	290
(1) *Via Gampola and Ramboda Pass.*	
(2) *Via Gampola, Nawalapitiya, Hatton, Maskeliya (Adam's Peak), and Talawakele. From Nuwara Eliya to Wellimada, Badulla, Bandarawela, Haputale, Haldumulla, Balangoda, Ratnapura, Avisawella, and Colombo.*	
INDEX	307

LIST OF ILLUSTRATIONS

☼

	FACING PAGE
1. THE REST-HOUSE, TANGALLA	32
2. THE REST-HOUSE, KEKIRAWA	33
3. THE REST-HOUSE, TISSAMAHARAMA	50
4. IATHALE DAGOBA, TISSAMAHARAMA	51
5. THE KANTAKA CETIYA, MIHINTALE. VIEW FROM THE NAGA POKUNA	112
6. THE "BRAZEN PALACE," ANURADHAPURA	113
7. THE "KING'S PALACE," ANURADHAPURA	128
8. MOONSTONE "KING'S PALACE," ANURADHAPURA	129
9. SEDENT BUDDHA, ANURADHAPURA	136
10. THE THUPARAMA, POLONNARUWA	137
11. THE LANKATILAKA, POLONNARUWA	140
12. SEDENT BUDDHA, GAL-VIHARA, POLONNARUWA	141
13. THE RECUMBENT BUDDHA, GAL-VIHARA, POLONNARUWA	148
14. THE ROYAL STAIRWAY, YAPAHUWA	149
15. SIGIRIYA	152
16. FRESCOES, SIGIRIYA	153
17. THE LION'S CLAW, SIGIRIYA	156
18. TEMPLE OF THE TOOTH, KANDY	157
19. ELEPHANTS IN RELIEF, ISURUMUNIYA	172
20. THE ALUVIHARE	173

Ceylon

	FACING PAGE
21. THE GEDI-GÉ	176
22. THE PREACHING BUDDHA, AUKANA VIHARA	177
23. LEOPARD AT THE KILL	192
24. THE LOWER ENTRANCE GATE, GALLE	193
25. THE "STAR" FORT, MATARA	224
26. ELEPHANTS BATHING IN THE NIL-GANGA	225
27. THE FORT, BATTICALOA	232
28. "SNAKE-BIRDS"	233
29. AN ANTHILL IN THE JUNGLE	264
30. THE "BIBLE" ROCK	265
31. HINDU TEMPLE, MUNESSERAM	288
32. BUFFALOES BATHING NEAR PUTTALAM	289
MAP OF CEYLON	304

Chapter One

INTRODUCTION TO CEYLON AND THE CEYLONESE

☼

The incidence that Ceylon is a country comparatively remote from all others, with the obvious exception of India, has served as a justification throughout the ages for the zealous traveller to keep a journal or to write a book. The first of these was the Chinese monk Fa-Hien, who in his pious search for traces of Buddha Gautama visited Ceylon about A.D. 400. On his return he wrote copiously about the "Master's" activities there, although historically he never once visited the island. Fa-Hien records, however, that at Anuradhapura he saw an image of Buddha in green jade, which was more than twenty cubits high. In the palm of the right hand lay a priceless pearl, and the image had "an appearance of solemn dignity which words cannot express." A hundred years later Sopater wrote of the famous ruby which had been erected on the tee of a Dagoba in the capital of Anuradhapura, which was like a "hyacinth, as large as a pine cone, the colour of fire . . ."

Ceylon

Seven hundred years later the ubiquitous Marco Polo arrived and was fascinated by the jewels of Ceylon, noting that the King possessed "the grandest ruby that was ever seen, a span in length, the thickness of a man's arm."

The first Englishman to write of the island was Robert Knox in his delightful *Historical Relation of Ceylon*. His visit was, however, fortuitous since he was shipwrecked off Trincomalee in 1660, and its duration was determined by the King, who held him a prisoner for twenty years. A less adventurous and more ingenuous visitor to Ceylon was Mrs. Heber, the wife of the Anglican bishop who, according to tradition, having once lost his luggage in the island, expressed his aggravation in those classic lines: "What though the spicy breezes, Blow soft on Ceylon's isle, Though every prospect pleases, And only man is vile." This lady, who visited Ceylon in 1825, when her husband was Bishop of Calcutta, and unaccountably refrained for nineteen years from writing her inevitable *Journal of a Tour to Ceylon*, would appear to have possessed a credulous mind. Alone amongst visitors to the island, she frequently encountered the "flying leech," which she wrote had "the power of springing, by means of a filament, to a considerable distance." Fortunately these bounding

Introduction to Ceylon and the Ceylonese

insects have, up to the present day, confined their activities to Mrs. Heber's person.

All these eminent travellers in the island, so diverse in nationality, period, and temperament, had one quality in common: they were too proud or too simple to attempt to justify their works on Ceylon. I propose, most humbly, to follow their illustrious example.

The name of the island, on the tongues of foreigners, has varied profoundly throughout the ages. To the ancient Greeks it was "Taprobane," which is a corruption of Tamil, meaning, I am assured, "The Pond covered with the Red Lotus." The Chinese called it "The Land without Sorrow" or "The Island of Jewels." The Mahommedan invaders from India, or Moors as they are loosely called, devised "Serendib," a corruption of "Sinhala Dvipa," meaning "Lion-dwelling Place" in the Singalese language, which the island was first called by the Singalese invaders, although no trace of a lion had ever been found there. The Portuguese in the sixteenth century changed "Serendib" into "Ceilao," although the two names appear to have no connection with each other; and the Dutch, in the following century, transformed with less imagination "Ceilao" into "Ceilon." A hundred and fifty years later it was anglicized by the English

Ceylon

invaders into "Ceylon." But to the inhabitants the island has been called "Lanka" for centuries, and such is it called by them to-day.

Although Buddhist poets have sung of Ceylon as "a pearl upon the brow of India," a cursory glance at the island on a map will show that, in geographical formation, it more resembles a liver. A liver, however, can be just as interesting as a pearl and, in the opinion of many, an even more precious possession. In area Ceylon is approximately one-third smaller than Ireland and, although lying under profoundly different climates, both islands enjoy a lush and variegated vegetation. But the historical similitude between them is even more curious and exact. Both have been oppressed for centuries by one or more alien races, and therefore they suffer the psychological consequences of having been subject races. But while the Irish have only been persecuted by the English, the Singalese have also been harried or dominated by the Portuguese and the Dutch, while the Tamils, a general name for the various marauding tribes from southern India, in a series of invasions, between the second century B.C. and the fourteenth century A.D., succeeded in dominating the northern half of the island, where they form the vast majority of the population to-day.

Introduction to Ceylon and the Ceylonese

A further interesting comparison can be drawn between the northern and southern inhabitants of Ceylon and Ireland. The Hindu Tamils introduced an alien religion into Buddhist Ceylon, just as the Scots foisted the Protestant religion on Catholic Ireland. In both cases the natives of the invaded islands considered the imported religion an erroneous and debased form of their own faith. Here, however, the religious comparison ends, since the Hindus and Buddhists have always been tolerantly disposed towards each other.

Apart from the Singalese, themselves an Indian tribe which occupied Ceylon about 500 B.C., and the Tamils, the other two important races in Ceylon are the Moors, who have traded on the coast for the last thousand years, and the Burghers, who are exclusively of Eurasian ancestry. The latter are descendants of the Portuguese or Dutch settlers who intermarried with the Singalese, and they are chiefly found in the larger towns of the island. The following figures will give the reader some idea of the races and religions of Ceylon; the figures are only approximate. Total population, 5,500,000.

3,500,000 Singalese. Buddhist in religion with a
   Christian minority.

Ceylon

1,300,000 Tamils. Hindu in religion with a similar Christian minority.

380,000 Moors, nearly all of whom are Muhammadans.

37,000 Burghers, exclusively Christian and mainly belonging to the Catholic Church.

555,000 Christians of all denominations, drawn from all races and including the European population. Three-quarters of the Christians are Roman Catholics.

Buddhism, which, as these statistics show, has the largest number of adherents in Ceylon, will be discussed in a later chapter, but for the convenience of the traveller I will here describe some of the salient characteristics and differences of the Singalese, Tamil, and Burgher races.

The significance of clothes in Ceylon is of primary importance, and the first thing that will strike the European visitor in this connection is the remarkable similarity between the sexes. This is principally the result of the ubiquitous "cloth," skirt-like in form, which is common to both men and women of the Singalese and Tamil races. The cloth worn by the Singalese male is called a *sarong*, and it is made in a coloured silk or cotton, often with a stripe. The *sarong* is shaped like a very

Introduction to Ceylon and the Ceylonese

wide petticoat and, when the wearer has stepped into it, the opposite corners are crossed over each other and tucked in tightly round the waist. Pins are never used to secure it, and a European would find it very difficult even to walk across the room without the *sarong* descending to his feet. Drawers are never worn under the *sarong*, nor under the *veti*, the Tamil equivalent of the former, although the *veti*, which are wound round the body, are always white and usually shorter than the *sarong*.

Another common attribute of the sexes amongst the Singalese and Tamils is the *konde*, or bun of hair, on the back of the head, which is kept in position by a gold or silver pin called the *konde-kura*. Unfortunately the *konde* is becoming rarer on men, although in the country it is still often worn. Even more rarely seen are the high tortoiseshell combs, at one time a common ornament to the men of the low country. European methods of hairdressing are causing havoc amongst the once picturesque heads of the Tamils and Singalese.

The top half of the male figure, when it is not naked, is now usually clothed with a white or coloured cloth thrown over the shoulders, while the legs and feet are always bare amongst Ceylonese of all classes who wear native costume. The reason for this, apart from climatic considerations, is

Ceylon

suggested by Robert Knox when he writes that shoes and stockings were a royal dress and only worn by the King. A contemporary picture of King Raja Sinha in the seventeenth century supports Knox's interesting assertion. The result in Ceylon to-day of this age-long custom is very remarkable and even comic in the case of the police. A huge Malayan constable on point duty (the police are usually drawn from Malay), dressed in pith helmet, khaki tunic and shorts, with bare legs, seems rather an incongruous figure in European eyes.

The clothes of the Singalese and Tamil female are of less importance than those of the male, since women in Ceylon, as elsewhere in the East, are far less in the public eye than men. The brightly coloured Indian *sahri* is worn by the more prosperous classes. This silken garment is wound round the body in the most elaborate folds with the loose end hanging over the right shoulder. If well put on over a good figure, this is a most attractive costume. The lower classes wear the ordinary cloth with a bodice, usually both of a sombre hue. Many ladies of Jaffna, however, make an exception to this rule by wearing together bright red and yellow garments. The cause of their affection for this strident combination of colours is unknown,

Introduction to Ceylon and the Ceylonese

as also its localization to the Jaffna peninsula. Some low-country women still dress in the white low-necked jacket trimmed with lace and reaching to the waist, which is a direct descendant of the indoor dress worn by Portuguese ladies in the sixteenth century. The majority of the women, however, whom the traveller will see in Ceylon will be carrying some packet or basket on their heads, usually of a domestic nature, which will remind him that in the East the first function of a woman is of a useful rather than of an ornamental character.

Burgher men, with their mixture of European and Singalese blood, all dress to-day in European clothes. But although they spurn native dress during the day, most of them sleep in the *sarong* rather than in pyjamas. When night falls it appears that the Eurasians of Ceylon tend to forget their Portuguese or Dutch ancestry. Burgher women are divided in their sympathies as regards Eastern and Western attire, although on the whole the *sahri* seems fortunately more popular than the coat and skirt. Burgher girls, however, usually wear European clothes until the age of sixteen, when with good sense they abandon them for the *sahri*. Except in this instance, an ever-increasing number of Ceylonese are copying the West both in clothes

Ceylon

and hairdressing. This growing tendency is greatly to be deplored, since no coloured race gains in either dignity or comfort by imitating the customs of Europe.

In a later paragraph, when discussing climatic conditions, I hope to make a general and I hope not invidious comment on the Ceylonese character, but here I would like to particularize on one aspect: the strength of superstition in the island, some manifestations of which the traveller is sure to encounter. Both Buddhists and Hindus are greatly influenced by omens. The cry of the lizard, commonly called the *ghekko*, they regard as most unlucky, and it deters them from making a decision. Sneezing is regarded in the same light. Deformed or invalided people are said to bring bad luck, but certainly in the seventeenth century, according to Robert Knox, the Singalese regarded "a white man or a big-bellied woman" as a most fortunate omen. Although both Singalese and Tamils are very clean people, they have a curious superstition regarding their ablutions. Every evening at sundown they wash themselves from head to foot, with the invariable exceptions of Tuesdays and Fridays. To wash on those days is thought most unlucky. I heard no explanation of the strange ban on these two days.

Introduction to Ceylon and the Ceylonese

There are also various superstitions regarding food, of which the most remarkable is the widespread belief that it is essential to drink water after eating meat, in order to expel the devil lurking in all flesh. Although this was originally a Hindu superstition, many Buddhists and Christians have long adopted it. It is also regarded as fatal to take fried meat on a journey up Adam's Peak, the famous mountain of pilgrimage in the south-west of the island. I have even been assured by an earnest Singalese Christian that on one occasion twelve Tamil men, who ignored this injunction, all died on the mountain. But I cannot vouch for the truth of this story, nor indeed explain the basis of this strange belief.

There is one superstition, however, which cannot be lightly dismissed as unworthy of European credence. I refer to the healing properties connected with "devil-dances." The dance which is staged for the benefit of the traveller is usually an empty, and always an expensive, ceremony. But when at night the tom-tom is heard in an adjacent village, mingled with the weird rhythmic singing of the inhabitants, it will probably signify a ceremony of healing. A well-known Tamil doctor, educated in Europe, once assured me of his reasoned belief in the possibility of cures

Ceylon

effected through the medium of "devil-dancing," and he said that often these had been substantiated after all Western methods of doctoring had failed. He even admitted that in some cases he allowed the relatives to remove a patient from hospital, with the avowed object of him being subjected to these occult practices. The authorities, he added, were aware of this custom but ignored it, unless the patient died outside hospital, when the doctor was held responsible. Many examples were given me by this distinguished physician of cures effected in his presence, and of these one in particular has remained in my memory. A male child, at the point of death with malarial fever, was taken from hospital by his mother and a "devil-dance" was organized for his benefit. During the ceremony the mother drove a skewer right through the boy's tongue. From that moment the fever rapidly subsided, and on inspection the doctor could find no mark of the skewer on the child's tongue, although he himself had witnessed its penetration. There are many such well-authenticated cures at "devil-dances," which bewilder Western understanding.

Such are some of the peculiarities and customs of the main Ceylonese races but, as climate is a dominating factor in human character, which largely moulds history, as also in vegetation which

Introduction to Ceylon and the Ceylonese

makes scenery, it is now necessary to understand something of the extreme and monotonous climate which rules in the island. Those gentle variations of the seasons which form the principal topic of conversation in this country are unknown in Ceylon, where perpetual summer prevails in so far as the temperature is concerned, except in the isolated hill country round Nuwara Eliya, where it is in general comparatively cool.

The climate of the island is regulated by two monsoons or winds: the south-west which arrives in May, and the north-east which brings torrential rains in October. But there is nothing in these rains, which last about two months, to stimulate either interest or anxiety. They are as inevitable as the sun which shines when the rains cease. But if these fixed periods of sunshine and rain—since in Ceylon a "drizzle" is unknown—account for the remarkable fertility of the soil and the grandeur and variety of the vegetation, they are also partly responsible for many qualities and defects in the Ceylonese character. The fixed seasons, ruled by the monsoons, and the perennial heat in a country where daylight and darkness divide with unvarying precision the twenty-four hours of the day, must necessarily produce in the character of the inhabitants a sense of monotony which they themselves

Ceylon

are unable to appreciate. Sunshine is liable to make a race happy, kindly, and irresponsible; but monotony destroys initiative and creates fatalism which, in the case of the Ceylonese, has been emphasized by the tenets of Buddhism. Most humbly I would suggest that such, in short, are the principal characteristics of the inhabitants of Ceylon; characteristics which in the main are the direct results of their agreeable but monotonous climate.

Fortunately for the sake of art, the deadening results of religion and weather were not effective for many hundreds of years after the arrival of the Singalese in Ceylon. Indeed, it was largely owing to the first-fruits of Buddhism in the island that about 200 B.C. the magnificent city of Anuradhapura was built, the ruins of which are the first archaeological interest of Ceylon to-day. For many centuries the city was rebuilt after successive Tamil raids, but it would appear from excavations always in a homogeneous style until, about A.D. 900, it was abandoned to the depredations of the invaders and the encroachment of the jungle. When Polonnaruwa was built in the twelfth century, to take the place of the older capital, the original architectural genius which had infused Anuradhapura was dead, since the ruins of Polon-

Introduction to Ceylon and the Ceylonese

naruwa, beautiful as they are, clearly indicate that where the style is not derivative it is inspired by the so-called "Dravidian" architecture of southern India. Traces of later originality may occasionally be discovered, but these cannot alter the remarkable incidence that the architectural and sculptural genius of the Singalese race reached its zenith approximately two thousand years ago.

The ruins of the "Lost Cities," the urban and scenic beauties, and the singular life of the jungle form a trinity of absorbing interests, one of which, if not all, is certain to appeal to an intelligent traveller. While the fact that Ceylon is compact in size and blessed with good roads and an amiable if inquisitive populace makes it possible to become well acquainted with the island in the course of a few months; provided energy and discernment are employed in that most delightful of occupations, "sight-seeing."

To-day it is said to be possible to "do" Ceylon in a fortnight, without venturing under any roof which does not cover a so-called first-class hotel. This claim can no doubt be justified as regards the more famous historical monuments, of which a superficial idea can be obtained in a day from the hotels at either Anuradhapura or Trincomalee, and the better-known towns such as Colombo, Kandy,

Ceylon

Nuwara Eliya, and Galle all possess at least one reasonable hotel. Such ignoble sight-seeing will undoubtedly satisfy those who wish to impress their English friends on their return with the difficult names of the ruined cities of Anuradhapura and Polonnaruwa, of the rock temples at Dambulla and of the rock palace at Sigiriya. After a fortnight in Ceylon they may have learnt to pronounce these names with doubtful accuracy, and in case their friends should be worried about their social connections in the island they can always reassure them with the information that at the Galle-Face Hotel in Colombo the Saturday night "cabaret-dance" is most exclusive and compares favourably with that at the Savoy in London.

A traveller of zeal and integrity must therefore disabuse himself of the notion that the varied interests of Ceylon can be leisurely inspected and truly appreciated with the background of comfort to which he is accustomed at home. The ruined cities and well-known towns which I have mentioned form but a part of the wealth of beauty and interest the island enjoys. Little-known ruins which are still being excavated or restored, villages which have remained unchanged in atmosphere since the days of the early Singalese kings, and above all the varied aspects of the jungle can only

Introduction to Ceylon and the Ceylonese

be enjoyed by those who are prepared to dispense with electric light, water sanitation, soft beds and European food. Indeed, the true significance of Ceylon can only be understood by the traveller who is willing to make frequent use of her rest-houses. It is not enough, however, that he should merely tolerate, probably with some self-satisfaction, the rather rudimentary comforts of these dwellings; he must also learn to understand and appreciate them at their true value. Before the mystery of the "Lost Cities" can be divined, or the religion of the Lord Buddha which inspired their creation, before Mihintale or Adam's Peak can be scaled, and above all before the life of the jungle can be studied and understood, it is essential to perceive the charm and indeed the importance of these diffuse and amiable institutions. For that reason I make no apology for entitling the next chapter of this book "The Rest-House."

Chapter Two

THE REST-HOUSE

☼

Perhaps the question should first be answered as to what a rest-house actually is, apart from the general indication given in the name that it must be some sort of edifice, presumably with a roof, where rest can be enjoyed at night or, if necessary, during the day.

Rest-houses were built, not for travellers of the past nor of to-day, but for the itinerant English officials of the last century who were not content with the more primitive bivouac which, with the exception of governors, had satisfied their Dutch predecessors. Government, having built these original rest-houses, carried on the responsibility, and in consequence all these buildings are owned by the municipal or urban authorities to-day; the officials themselves being housed in possibly less attractive but more convenient localities. I hope to show in the course of this chapter that there is no better argument in favour of government control in general than the rest-houses of Ceylon.

The appellation of "rest-house," therefore, in-

The Rest-House

variably denotes the ownership of the local authorities, while that of "hotel" means that the building is in private hands. This, however, does not imply that an hotel must be preferable to a rest-house. Indeed, with the rare exceptions of the large towns where good hotels make rest-houses superfluous, the latter are intended for Europeans and the more opulent Ceylonese; while the local village hotel, often boasting a grandiloquent name, usually consists of one large windowless room above a shop, or *boutique* as it is called in Ceylon, with no sleeping accommodation but a roll of coconut matting. I will now briefly describe the typical structure and arrangements of an average rest-house situated in the more remote parts of the island.

A short drive, either of red dust or yellow gravel, leads to a low bungalow of simple construction with a roof of concave red tiles lined with the leaves of the palmyra palm. There is no entrance door, and one walks up a few steps straight into the living-room, a large square space raised on a stone platform about three feet from the ground, and open to the elements on three sides. On arrival you observe with relief that there is no light in the rest-house nor car under the porch, since strange company in such a restricted

Ceylon

space is apt to be oppressive although, in my experience, comparatively rare.

As I have suggested, it is inevitably evening when you arrive to spend the night at a rest-house, and in Ceylon it is always dark by half-past six. Your first gesture on entering is to shout "Boy," hoarsely owing to lack of refreshment, and soon a running figure will appear struggling into his white linen coat, which Government insists should be worn by rest-house keepers to receive their guests. After having expressed your desire for accommodation, or maybe only for a drink, other figures will emerge from the darkness bearing oil lamps which illuminate for your inspection the rest of the building. From the far corners of the living-room extend two short wings, each of which contains one or more high and very simple bedrooms. These are naturally in darkness, but the lamps disclose a wide verandah in front of the rooms protected by a sloping roof. This is the most typical and charming portion of the rest-house and forms an extension to your bedroom or, if you desire to avoid the communal living-room, a space in which to dine alone.

The light carried by the "boy" towards your bedroom also discloses in the verandah a unique product of Ceylon: the ubiquitous rest-house

1. The Rest-house, Tangalla

2. *The Rest-house, Kekirawa*

The Rest-House

chair. This contraption (it deserves no better appellation) is formed of a crushed semi-circle of the hardest cane, and it is provided with straight teak arms to prevent the European figure from slipping over the edge. Under these arms are concealed two long splats, which should be immediately extended on taking your seat, as by twisting the legs over their unyielding surface you may be able to retain your precarious hold on the chair. While engaged in this arduous manœuvre, the rest-house keeper will be suggesting that you should dine off soup from a bottle, a chicken which will be caught, killed and cooked for you in the short space of an hour, and tinned fruit to conclude this appetizing meal. If you are prudent, you will instantly decline all these proposals and demand a rice and curry, begging, if you are a novice, that it should not be made too hot. The rest-house keeper will probably smile at you with indulgence or incredulity, but you will be well advised to insist.

After settling this point the traveller may feel inclined to inspect his bedroom, and perhaps at first glance it may impress him unfavourably if he is unaccustomed to rest-house furniture. There will be two iron bedsteads in the room, either at opposite ends or side by side, according to the

Ceylon

requirements of the last occupants. On each bed will lie a mattress of coconut fibre and a folded mosquito net; nothing more. There may or may not be a chair, but there will certainly be a dressing-table with a glass but no drawers. Your bag will be placed on a pedestal, which on inspection will prove to be empty.

The rest-house keeper will then show you the bathroom, probably with considerable pride. Every bedroom in a rest-house possesses a bathroom leading out of it, usually of a primitive nature, which is divided into two by a four-foot concrete wall. In the larger bathing portion there will possibly be nothing but a small bucket, and looking over the partition you will notice a pail with a wooden lid, since earth rather than water is the invariable method of sanitation. In the rainy season you will probably see one or more frogs croaking round the pail. You should not, however, be discouraged unless you observe by the light of the candle, which will be standing on a plate on the top of the partition wall, the presence of a spider, a scorpion or a centipede, when it will be advisable to send for the "boy." The spider will probably be harmless, unless his legs are enveloped in fur, in which case he may be a tarantula with the power of inflicting a deadly wound. The scorpion

The Rest-House

is also vicious and can inject a most dangerous poison, while the bite of a centipede causes an immense swelling and acute pain for twenty-four hours. If, however, the latter should prove on inspection to be a millepede, a long golden insect with presumably a thousand legs, no apprehension need be entertained. This creature is harmless and can be tamed at will.

Having finished the examination of the bathroom, it is advisable to order your bath immediately, since it often takes as long to fill a bath as to bring the curry, which anyhow cannot be prepared much under an hour. Whether you order a warm or a cold bath will probably prove immaterial, since cold water is often indistinguishable from warm in Ceylon. A small tin bath will then be pulled into the bathroom, and at long intervals small buckets of water will be poured into it by the "boy." It is advisable to have your bath immediately it is ready, otherwise you will share it with innumerable black-beetles, although, owing to the feeble light given by the candle, these insects may mercifully be invisible. The use of the small bucket left in the bathroom may now become apparent; you are expected to pour water from it over your body, as it is thought unlikely by the local authorities that you will possess a sponge.

Ceylon

Your dinner in the living-room, or on the verandah in front of your bedroom, should be a revelation if you have learnt to eat curry. Country rice with a brown tinge will be provided in this rest-house, as it is small and remote, and many prefer it to the white and long-grained "table" rice from India. There will probably be at least six different curries to lay reverently on the top of your foundation of rice: chicken, meat and egg curries in the country, and prawns if you are near the sea; drum-sticks, ladies' fingers, bread-fruit, and dahl will be the most likely vegetables, and there is certain to be a sambol of onions and a brown sambol paste of coconuts and chili, which the novice should eat sparingly. The mountain of food which now lies on your plate should then be covered with a thick layer of grated coconut, and a poppadum should be by your side before you begin this delicious dinner. Perched on one corner of the large table stands the primitive oil-lamp, which throws an oscillating light on the meal, and it will be enveloped in a film of dying insects—mosquitoes, beetles, and crickets predominating—while its presence prohibits the use of the red-fringed rep punkah above your head which, if at luncheon, would be lackadaisically pulled by an impish wallah, gazing at you with bright and

The Rest-House

inquisitive eyes. Having finished your dinner, you will be little tempted to stay up late, since a solitary lamp is a depressing form of illumination, particularly when it is clouded with predatory insects. Some of these, however, including the tic and the "eye-fly" (so called after the incorrect supposition that it assaults the human eye), will abandon the lamp for the floor, where they will feast contentedly on your lower limbs.

Once in bed under the mosquito net, you will be able to enjoy in safety the variegated nocturnal noises of Ceylon. You need have no fear of a leopard or bear disturbing your privacy, as the rest-house will be surrounded by a fence of barbed wire, which will enable you to keep your bedroom door open on to the verandah. Naturally the buzz of the frustrated mosquito outside the net will first attract your attention, or perhaps the croak of the frog, which has returned to its usual habitat after being disturbed by your bath. You may next be startled by the sudden howl of a pack of jackals in full cry in the close vicinity of the rest-house. This is a most eerie sound, and as it rises in a vicious crescendo you may, as a novice, throw an anxious glance towards the open door. Then at the high pitch of ferocity the howl stops sharply, like the violins in an orchestra after a fortissimo

Ceylon

passage—yet with this difference: after a few beats the music would continue, but the jackals remain silent, having secured their prey.

While you are wondering what species of animal they are devouring (it will probably be a faun or a mouse-deer) your mind will be directed to the immediate neighbourhood by the shrill cry of the *ghekko* on the wall above your bed. This amiable little lizard is ubiquitous in Ceylon, and while he chases the flies he emits the sound described in his onomatopoeic nickname. This noise is friendly and comforting and a good accompaniment to sleep, although the Ceylonese, as I have mentioned, regard it as most unlucky. Indeed, they advise that any decision must instantly be abandoned on hearing the *ghekko*. As, however, his cries are often intermittent from sunset to dawn it might prove inconvenient, even during the night, to follow this wary counsel.

You will clearly arise early, having gone to bed at nine, and on walking on to the verandah you will almost certainly be enchanted with the splendid situation of the rest-house. If on the coast, it will be perched on the edge of a sandy promontory overlooking a grey sea, which gradually turns aquamarine under the touch of dawn. If in the hinterland, a spacious lake will lie below

The Rest-House

you, either at the very door of the rest-house or else visible through a short vista of shimmering palm-trees. Its silver waters turning pink with the rising sun may reveal a host of black cormorants or snow-white cranes. Even if you have spent the night in a rest-house in the heart of the jungle, the undergrowth around will have been cleared away, and through the rope-like arms of the silver banyan-trees you will obtain a distant view of high mountains in deep shade. The bygone officials who selected the sites for the Ceylonese rest-houses were gifted with a singular genius, and once more, if not too hidebound, you will feel grateful for government control.

For breakfast you can obtain bacon and eggs, and perhaps "Oxford" marmalade; but if you want a change from that conventional fare, you can easily be served with *hoppers*. This national dish, although excellent, does not present a very appetizing appearance, since the individual *hoppers* rather resembles the head of a putrefying toadstool. The centre, which is white and podgy, is formed of flour and "toddy," the latter being a form of liquor distilled from the coconut, and round this opaque nucleus there is a glutinous fringe of flour. The *hopper* should be eaten with a hot sambol of chili paste and coconut or, by the

Ceylon

craven-hearted, with jam. A less exacting Ceylonese dish for breakfast is *pitu*. This is a mixture of rice and flour which has been boiled in an empty bamboo over a steaming pot. After cooking it is ejected from the bamboo and cut up like long French bread.

While the visitor is eating *hoppers* and *pitu*, or more likely bacon and eggs, he will have time to observe the creatures in the immediate vicinity, and he may be interested to notice that the only two which appear identical both in England and Ceylon are the house fly and the sparrow. The former is the similar ubiquitous pest, but the Singalese make a remarkable claim for the sparrow, or "paddy-bird" as it is called in the island, owing to its prevalence in the rice-fields. They maintain that the sparrow satisfies its urge to procreation once in every five minutes and that, as a natural consequence, "paddy-bird" soup is freely drunk by childless men.

Another creature, unknown in England, may probably arrest your attention during breakfast. This is the *hikanella*, an olive-coloured lizard with two black stripes down its back. Its skin is similar in texture to that of a snake, and it is colloquially known as the "snake's" servant, since its appearance is supposed to indicate the approach of a

The Rest-House

cobra. It is improbable, however, that your breakfast will be disturbed by this beautiful hooded reptile, which would never attack, unless you were so imprudent as to tread on its tail. Your attention may next be drawn to the banyan-tree a few yards away, which overshadows the rest-house. Only the trunk is visible from where you are sitting, and on this knotted surface you will notice a motionless chameleon, occasionally protruding a long silver tongue as it devours some invisible fly. Above him two palm-squirrels romp round the tree. These amusing little animals are about the size of an egg, and possess a rapid clockwork movement reminiscent of the nursery. Their drab grey backs are relieved by three yellow stripes down the body, which are of legendary origin. When the god Rama was employed in building Adam's Bridge, one active squirrel assisted him in this arduous enterprise by rolling, and thus collecting sand in his coat, which he then rubbed between the stones to bind them together. In reward for this service Rama stroked the intelligent creature with three of his godly fingers, leaving the impress on his back which we see on the bodies of his descendants to-day.

You should by now have finished your breakfast, perhaps with an emerald-green papaw or a purple-

Ceylon

skinned mangosteen and, on receiving your bill, you are once again able to study the advantages and vagaries of Government control. *En pension* terms do not exist in rest-houses, and you are charged in the first place for "occupation"; not necessarily of a bed, but even of a chair in which you may have spent only one uncomfortable hour, although with justice the chair is less expensive than the bed. The charge for occupation, in my opinion very moderate, goes to the local authorities who, as I have said, own and maintain the rest-house, while all profits on meals and drinks are the perquisites of the host. Although this system may appear quite fair, it has one result disadvantageous to the visitor. In larger rest-houses, where clients are more frequent, the rest-house keeper is soon able to make a substantial profit, and therefore he sometimes becomes indifferent to the comfort of his guests. It would be invidious to mention names in this connection, but after the experience gained by staying in nearly thirty rest-houses I usually tried to avoid those in the larger towns. In the smaller ones, such as we are now considering, I invariably enjoyed comfort and courtesy.

After paying most moderately for "occupation," food, drink, and linen (the two latter you can

The Rest-House

bring if you wish), you may be surprised to read on the printed bill that for "stabling" you are charged twenty-five cents. Not having brought your horses, you may be for a moment bewildered until on explanation you realize you are being asked to pay for the garaging of your car. You should then experience a sense of gratitude towards the conservatism of the local authorities which allows such a pleasing anachronism to persist. You will now tip the rest-house keeper, if he has waited on you, and reward him with only a bow if he has not, and you should drive away with feelings of regret, possibly tempered by satisfaction, at your unforeseen abilities to "rough it" with comparative ease.

Such are the experiences likely to be encountered in the smaller rest-houses, but their individual sites and characteristics I propose to describe later in this book, when I accompany the indulgent traveller on a few journeys through Ceylon. Until that moment arrives, a happy one at least to the author, I shall amuse myself, and I hope the reader, by relating a few anecdotes of my sojourns in various rest-houses, which may evoke pleasant memories amongst those who know Ceylon, and serve as an encouragement or warning to potential visitors who do not.

Ceylon

I was staying one night in a remote rest-house in the north central province when, as I was going to bed, my host, who was a Tamil, came and asked me if I had ever seen a cobra. I replied that I had not, except in the hands of a snake-charmer; so he invited me to come to his fowl-house, where a cobra had just killed some chickens together with the hen which had attempted to defend them. I followed him to the back of the rest-house, where by the light of torches held by the "boys" I observed a large black reptile crawling leisurely along by the wall. My host then armed himself with a large stick, a gesture which showed he was not a Buddhist, and asked me if "Master" would mind if he said a prayer before attacking the snake. I answered that, on the contrary, I thoroughly approved of his pious suggestion. Accordingly, he said a short prayer and crossed himself, a movement which proclaimed the Tamil to be of the Catholic faith. As the man approached the cobra to cut off its retreat, it rose a foot or more from the ground, displaying the famous hood, so often portrayed in Buddhist art. The torches which the "boys" were playing on it brightly illuminated this beautiful and courageous snake.

At this juncture I offered to fetch my gun, which I felt even in my obtuse hands might be a

The Rest-House

more safe and humane method of destroying the cobra. But as I spoke the rest-house keeper aimed a horizontal blow at its head, which the snake dexterously avoided and, with a hiss, struck at its assailant's arm, but fortunately with no greater success. I then hastily left the scene of action, determined to be armed myself for any further stages of the struggle and, on my return, I was greatly relieved to find that the snake was dead, the second blow of the rest-house keeper having been more accurate than the first. The black length of the cobra lay before me with the body below the head beaten into a pulp. My host then showed me the corpse of the hen and the bite which had killed her, just above the right leg. He pointed out that she could have escaped, but preferred to defend her young. I praised the bird's courage and his own, while he told me with emotion how he had cherished that particular fowl. He made a practice, he added, of choosing the names of his farmyard animals from the Roman Missal, and he had called the defunct hen Maria.

Not long afterwards I had another experience where a hen was concerned, although under totally different circumstances. I was staying in a rest-house on the east coast of the island. In size it was as small, and in position as remote, as any I

Ceylon

had seen. Visitors had been so rare that on my arrival one of the only two bedrooms had to be thoroughly swept before I could occupy it. In this there was nothing unusual, and the room was soon made spotlessly clean. But clearly amongst the previous occupants, or at least frequenters, of the room had been a brick-coloured hen since, on waking up the following morning, I observed this bird, through the mosquito net, in a crouching position by my bed. Being unused to hens in the bedroom, I clapped my hands at her and she stalked slowly out, clucking in protest at my behaviour. A short time later I went to the bathroom; it was about six o'clock, the normal time to arise in the jungle, but nevertheless an hour at which in my case neither mind nor sight function rapidly. I was, however, somewhat disturbed about the state of these organs when, on inspecting the pail for spiders or centipedes, it appeared to me to contain a feathered occupant.

I returned to my bedroom and hastily looked across the sea in order to clear my eyes, but the same unusual spectacle greeted them on my return to the bathroom. I then called the "boy," and in my agitation addressed him in the same manner I should have adopted to the housemaid in an English station hotel. "If I am not mistaken," I said, "there

The Rest-House

seems to me to be a hen in the pail in the bathroom. Would you, perhaps, be kind enough to remove it?" Naturally the "boy" did not understand and, after twice repeating this courteous request with no result, it occurred to me that a shorter sentence and a less oblique reference to the position assumed by the hen might prove more effective. So I tried him briefly with "Fowl in closet. Take away at once!" The "boy" understood with his ears, but his mind could not immediately grapple with such an unusual situation, so I led him into the bathroom and pointed out the offending bird. The "boy" laughed heartily at the sight, and although I did not join in his hilarity I willingly forgave him. Then with care and affection he picked out of the pail the brick-coloured hen which I had so rudely chased from my bedside. While I was feeling some compunction at having twice disturbed her the "boy" again broke into loud laughter, since inspection proved that in the bottom of the pail this eccentric bird had laid an egg.

An experience with more sentiment than humour happened to me at the first rest-house in which I stayed in Ceylon. Shortly after dinner I had taken a drive and, within a mile of the rest-house, I had seen a leopard strolling down the roadside in that direction. Timidity, I hope not

Ceylon

altogether unnatural, induced me to inquire from my host on my return whether it was safe to leave my door open on to the verandah, since suffocation was, in my opinion, preferable to a nocturnal visit from the leopard. The man laughed indulgently and assured me that no animal other than the jackal, which despises human beings unless already dead, had ever been known to enter the compound. As I was still unconvinced the rest-house keeper said he would lend me "Coffee" for the night, and left me wondering what creature this might be. But he shortly returned with a black and melancholy dog, which in the light of the solitary lamp, appeared to be a cross between an Alsatian and a Manchester terrier. Closer inspection proved that some ten years previously she must have been a mother. "Master!" said the rest-house keeper, pointing firmly in my direction, and left for the night. As soon as the sound of his footsteps had faded down the verandah, "Coffee" approached me with leisurely curiosity and smelt my leg; then she looked up at me with large brown eyes which, although reflecting a sense of duty, were quite impersonal in their regard. Meanwhile I had refrained from any tangible endearment, remembering the nursery maxim, "Never pat a strange dog."

The Rest-House

As soon as "Coffee" left me to take up a central position in the bedroom I began to unpack, but I noticed that her eyes followed me everywhere. Having finished, I went into the bathroom and shut the door. A few seconds later I heard a determined scratch outside, and I hastened to let "Coffee" in. She watched me with the same blank stare as I performed my modest ablutions and followed me back to my room where, on my turning out the lamp, she settled down under the bed. I was at that time unused to the varied and startling noises of the jungle and in consequence I slept badly and, whenever I reawoke after a short period of sleep, I at once mistook "Coffee's" heavy breathing for that of some wild animal. Also in the course of the night "Coffee" twice left the bedroom barking furiously, and although she soon returned, apparently reassured in her own mind, I could not fully share her complacency. Early in the morning after a most restless night "Coffee" growled angrily when I attempted to leave my bed, but whether this was a danger signal or merely an indication of her resentment at being disturbed I never discovered, since I remained in bed.

Eventually to my relief the dog was removed by a "boy," which enabled me to spend the

Ceylon

morning visiting an important historical monument nearby, to which I drove in a car. On leaving the rest-house, "Coffee" walked with me as far as the gate and, after declining my invitation to accompany me, she sat in the middle of the road watching my departure with discouraging eyes. On my return she was waiting at the gate to receive me and preceded me to the verandah where my luncheon had been laid. During the meal she chased away a chicken, two squirrels, and a chameleon which, in her opinion, had approached too close to the table, but she despised all the tit-bits with which I had hoped to stimulate her affection.

After luncheon I had to do my packing, and I was surprised, even rather annoyed, by "Coffee's" persistency in standing in my way, although naturally I did not dare to rebuke her. When I had finished and was about to close my suit-case "Coffee," to my great astonishment, unbent for the first time during our brief intimacy. She put her paws on the trestle on which lay my bag, she looked up at me with kindly eyes, she whined, she even wagged her tail. I have never felt more flattered in my life. I later heard a distressing rumour that "Coffee" had been devoured by a leopard. If so, she must have proved a tough

3. The Rest-house, Tissamaharama

4. *Iathale Dagoba, Tissamaharama (See page 110)*

The Rest-House

morsel even for a leopard to chew, and I am sure that she looked at death courageously with those sad, dispassionate eyes.

Rest-house stories, which are legion amongst travellers in Ceylon, can vary from the obscene to the ridiculous, but they are all founded on the unexpected humour and unconscious charm of the human and animal life in the island. To appreciate the true significance of the rest-house is therefore the first step for the enlightened traveller towards acquiring an understanding and love of Ceylon.

Chapter Three

THE LORD BUDDHA

✦

Some chronicle of the life of Buddha Gautama, and of the religion which bears his name, is essential to an understanding of the Singalese kings and of the "Lost Cities," which were built for religious rather than for monarchical or civic motives. This account must inevitably be brief, but will, I hope, be of use to the average visitor whose knowledge of Buddhism and its founder may be on arrival in Ceylon more nebulous than precise, as indeed was my own.

In history, as apart from legend, the later "Buddha," or "Enlightened One," was born Prince Siddhartha Gautama, the son of the Hindu King Suddhodana of the Sakyas and of the latter's wife, Queen Maya. His birthplace was Kapilavastu on the borders of Nepal, but the actual date has always been a matter of controversy. Professor Wilhelm Geiger, however, in his introduction to the Mahawamsa, states with authority that the Prince was born in 563 B.C. At sixteen he was married to Princess Yasodara, who gave birth to

The Lord Buddha

a son called Rahula; but at twenty-nine Prince Siddhartha renounced the world and became a hermit. At thirty-five he became "Buddha," or the "Enlightened One," his spiritual rebirth being called "Bodhi." The following forty-five years the Buddha spent propagating his doctrines in India, and he died in 483 B.C. at the age of eighty. Such is the dry historical sequence of the life of this momentous being, but the legends concerning him are naturally more picturesque, and some perhaps no less true than history.

Before Queen Maya gave birth it was prophesied that her child would become a Buddha, and one night she dreamt that he descended into her womb in the shape of a white elephant. This legend accounts for the Buddhist belief that a white elephant is the first of all animals, while a further legend that Buddha was born in a pleasure garden under a lotus-tree made this flower sacred to his followers. In Buddhist art the lotus is most general in all floral designs, and it is carved on the soles of the bare feet of all recumbent Buddhas.

Despite the pleasant surroundings of his youth and the company of a beautiful wife, Prince Siddhartha was often troubled by his reflections on the sorrows of humanity and, one day, accom-

Ceylon

panied by his favourite charioteer Channa, he visited the more squalid regions of the great city of Kapilavastu and, on his return to the palace, he announced his decision to forswear the world and to become a hermit. Neither threats nor cajolery could deter him, and one night he planned to leave the city on the back of his beloved horse Kanthaka. Unfortunately King Suddhodana heard rumours of his son's outrageous intention and ordered the gates of Kapilavastu to be closed. But friends contrived the opening of the gates, and complacent "Yakkhas" (witch-mares in Hindu mythology) supported the hoofs of Kanthaka, so that no clatter should disturb the sleeping city. So took place the "Great Departure," as it is known in both Buddhist annals and art.

Having escaped from the trammels of his royal position, Prince Siddhartha discarded his princely clothes for the orange robes of a hermit, similar to those worn by the *Bhikkhus* to-day, and sought holiness with a begging bowl in his hand and his mind concentrated on the discovery of truth. After six years of asceticism the Prince decided that the only spiritual path to pursue was that of independent meditation. Therefore at the age of thirty-five he sat for forty-nine days at the foot of a fig-tree in the forests of Orawela, in the

The Lord Buddha

present Princedom of Bihar, being protected, when necessary, from the sun and rain by the hood of a devout cobra. At length, after withstanding the attacks of Mara (Satan) and his flocks of fair daughters, the Prince received "Enlightenment" and became the "Buddha." The tree under which his spiritual rebirth took place was called the "Bodhi" or "Bo-tree," the most famous and sacred tree of the Eastern world.

Even legends record little of the forty-five years of Buddha's ceaseless propagation of the "Four Noble Truths," which will be discussed later. His mission, it is written, was inaugurated in the Deer Park at Benares, an incident represented in Buddhist art by the "Wheel of the Law," and during his missionary travels through North India occurred his two recorded "miracles." Buddha possessed, in company with many less important people, an undesirable cousin in the person of one Devadatta, who, jealous of his piety, loosened a rogue elephant called Nalagiri against him. But as soon as the beast felt the impress of the "Master's" hand it knelt down and did homage to him. The second so-called miracle concerned a monkey, which quenched Buddha's thirst in the desert with a goblet of palm-wine. Subsequently, overwhelmed by the honour, the pious monkey

Ceylon

plunged to his death in an adjacent well, to be rewarded for this suicidal action by instant rebirth in Heaven.

During Buddha's missionary labours legend, but not history, recounts that he visited Ceylon. Indeed, the Mahawamsa, the chronicle of the "greater" dynasty of Singalese kings, relates that the "Conqueror, in the ninth year of his Buddhahood . . . himself set forth for the isle of Lanka, to win Lanka for the faith." There the "Master" at first encountered resistance from the "Yakkhas," a name, in this case meaning demons, which the Singalese gave to the aboriginal inhabitants of Ceylon. But Buddha called a meeting of the "Yakkhas," at which "hovering in the air over their heads . . . he struck terror to their hearts by rain, storm, darkness and so forth." Naturally the "Yakkhas" were forced by these alarming portents to listen to Buddha, and "When he had destroyed their terror, cold and darkness, and had spread his rug of skin on the ground . . . the Conqueror, sitting there made the rug to spread wide, while burning flame surrounded it." The "Yakkhas" hastened to accept the doctrines of the "Master," and their Prince pleaded with Buddha for something they might worship after he had left them. So "the Conqueror, he who had pure

The Lord Buddha

and blue-black locks, passing his hand over his head, bestowed on him a handful of hairs. And he (the Prince) receiving this in a splendid gold urn, when he had laid the hairs upon a heap of many-coloured gems, seven cubits round, piled up at the place where the Master had sat, he covered them over with a *thupa* (mound) of sapphires and worshipped them." Unfortunately this picturesque account of Buddha's last action before leaving is entirely legendary, since historians assert he never once visited the island.

The last scene in the life of Buddha Gautama took place, as has been mentioned, in 483 B.C. at Kusinava, where the famous act of "Nirvana" was consummated. The Mahawamsa records the event as follows: "When the Conqueror, the incomparable, he who has the five eyes, had lived eighty-four years, and had fulfilled all his duties in the world in all ways, then at Kusinava in the holy place between the two Sala-trees, on the full-moon day of the month Vesakha (May) was the light of the world extinguished." The five eyes to which reference is made are the bodily eyes, the heavenly eye, the eye of understanding, the eye of omniscience, and finally the Buddha-eye by means of which he held the saving truth. As the "Nirvana" was an incident of more religious than historical

Ceylon

importance, it can be more easily discussed during the following section on the teaching of Buddha.

The Buddhist confession of faith consists of "Buddha, Dhamma and Samgha," the Buddha, his doctrine, and his community. The first has been considered, and the second rests on the "Four Noble Truths" expounded by Buddha in the deer park at Benares. These are: (1) Suffering. (2) The origin of suffering. (3) Extinction of suffering. (4) The eight-fold path to attain that end. Suffering is caused by ignorance and desire, and these can only be crushed and "Enlightenment" attained by following the "Noble Eight-fold Path," which enjoins an ethical attitude towards: (1) The understanding. (2) Aspirations. (3) Speech. (4) Actions. (5) Livelihood. (6) Effort. (7) Concentration. (8) Meditation. In treading this path, by which suffering is overcome, the individual will endure metapsychosis, or successive earthly embodiments, until perfection is acquired. Animal embodiments of the human entity are credited by Buddhists, a belief which accounts for their aversion to taking life in any form. Indeed, a good Buddhist will flick a chair with his handkerchief before sitting down, in order not to run the risk of killing a fly, while the drinking water of a priest

The Lord Buddha

or *bhikkhu* is always carefully strained to avoid his consuming any invisible life.

When "Enlightenment" is at length reached, by means of the "Noble Eight-fold Path," the entity is admitted into "Nirvana," which is a condition-not of spiritual extinction, as is sometimes supposed, but of the merging of the spirit into the Infinite Good. Death is no indication that Buddhahood has been attained, although "Nirvana" can only obtain with bodily death. Buddha Gautama was exceptional in reaching Buddhahood without entering into "Nirvana," but the "Master" separated these normally coetaneous spiritual experiences by a span of fifty years, in order that the world might profit from his doctrines and the contemplation of his saintly life.

Buddhism does not claim a divine foundation like Christianity. It is rather a deification of the human intellect, and in its commendable toleration of other religions Buddhism resembles a benevolent agnosticism. Nevertheless, Buddhists believe in "Lokas," or heavens and hells where, between transmigrations, reward or punishment is received by the individual spirit. Finally it must be remembered that in Buddhism there is no worship of a Supreme Being, nor did Buddha claim in any way to be God. Indeed, in the

Ceylon

"Dhamma" he is not even considered unique as a human being, since it is said that there were twenty-four Buddhas before the advent of Buddha Gautama, and he himself was the fourth in the present "Kalpa," or chronological period. It is also maintained that his doctrines will endure five thousand years from his "Nirvana," after which time the "Maitreya," or Saviour, will appear on earth. The latter is always represented in Buddhist art holding a vase of ambrosia in his right hand.

"Samgha," the corporate body of Buddhists, is mainly illustrated for the traveller by the temples, which are discussed later, and by the individual *bhikkhu* or Buddhist priest. These highly decorative personages in their bright yellow or orange gowns can be met at every turn of the road in Ceylon, and indeed if you are not a Buddhist, it is considered most unlucky to encounter one. But the visitor will welcome these men who, with their mild eyes and shaven heads, seem to exemplify the more pleasing aspects of their colourful but ascetic religion. The tenets of their faith compel them to beg for their food and, together with the talipot palm with which they protect their heads from sun and rain, the *bhikkhu's* bowl is the most conspicuous of his few possessions. Often the traveller will observe an orange-clad figure holding

The Lord Buddha

out his bowl, with averted eyes, at some house door. Soon the pious owner emerges, the bowl is filled with rice, and the *bhikkhu* disappears to enjoy his meal.

Further and more plentiful opportunities to satisfy his appetite are afforded to the *bhikkhu* by the different festivals in the Buddhist calendar. On these occasions all the edible offerings, in the form of fruit and vegetables, which are laid at the feet of the various statues of the Buddha are later consumed by the priests. "Wesak" provides a rare chance for such a feast, and it takes place on the first full moon in May. This festival not only celebrates Buddha's "Nirvana," but also his birth and attainment to Buddhahood, since these three momentous events occurred, according to his followers, on the same day of each year concerned. Fortunate is the traveller who finds himself in the island for "Wesak," as every Buddhist house is decorated for the occasion, and the altars reflect the general happiness by their piles of aromatic flowers and delectable fruit and vegetables.

To call a *bhikkhu* a priest, however, as is done in all European languages, is liable to cause an entire misapprehension as to his functions in the Buddhist community. The appellation "priest" signifies to a Christian a man who claims or

Ceylon

possesses sacrificial or sacramental faculties. These elements are wholly alien to Buddhism, and indeed the only pastoral office exercised by the *bhikkhu* is that of preaching, since even marriages are performed by the lay authorities. As a preacher, however, the *bhikkhu* excels, and neither he nor his congregation appear to consider a four hours' sermon to err on the side of verbosity.

The culmination of a *bhikkhu's* bodily existence is his funeral, since by one incident at this ceremony his spiritual condition on death can be appraised by even the humblest member of his community. A high funeral pyre is erected, in the middle of which the corpse is placed on a stretcher for cremation. Above the pyre the *bhikkhu's* orange robe is extended from the branches of neighbouring trees, and should the robe escape the flames, it is believed that the dead man's spiritual entity has attained to Buddhahood and passed into "Nirvana." Should the robe be burnt, however, then the mourners must reluctantly accept the evidence that further metapsychosis is necessary. I was once privileged to attend the funeral of a *bhikkhu* aged ninety, whose piety encouraged the hope that his robe would escape the flames. When the fire was lighted, however, the robe was instantly consumed, but owing to

The Lord Buddha

its close proximity to the pyre it appears to me that only divine intervention could have saved it from destruction.

"Buddha, Dhamma and Samgha," which can only be briefly considered in these pages, form a trinitarian confession of faith of a unique character in the history of religions, and their wide significance dominates the spiritual and material life of Ceylon.

Chapter Four

a. THE MAHAWAMSA, or THE GREATER DYNASTY

b. THE SULAWAMSA, or THE LESSER DYNASTY

☼

(a) The Mahawamsa

Having examined the religion which created the spiritual life and inspired the artistic creations of the island, the more important rulers of Ceylon, who were responsible for these factors, will now be considered.

Legend relates that the first King of Ceylon, Vijaya I, was the grandson of a lion. It is perhaps as likely as the tale that our Saxon kings were descended from a pig. In any case, "Sihala" means a lion and accounts for the name, if not for the origin, of the Singalese race. Tradition says that about 600 B.C. the King of Bengal had a daughter who, according to the chronicles called the Rajaviliya, "maddened by lust, descended privily at night from the upper storey" of the palace and

The Mahawamsa, or the Greater Dynasty

made the acquaintance of a passing lion. The creature, the Mahawamsa, the oldest of the Singalese chronicles, records, "roused to fiercest passion by her touch, took her upon his back and bore her with all speed to his cave. There he was united with her, and from this union with him the Princess in time bore twin children, a son and a daughter."

The hands and feet of this son, named Sihabahu, were formed like those of a lion and, having reached the age of sixteen, he inquired, without much sense of observation: "Wherefore are you and our father so different, dear Mother?" Scandalized by the information he received, Sihabahu removed his mother and sister from the cave and, clothing themselves with the branches of trees, they took refuge with the uncle of the Princess. Meanwhile the lion, not unnaturally incensed by the conduct of his family, ravaged the countryside until the King offered his very kingdom to the man who should slay such a dangerous beast. Thus it happened that Sihabahu went out to kill his father who, "on hearing his son's voice, was delighted as if nectar had been poured into his ears." Alas for filial duty! Sihabahu slew his father with a bow and arrow and obtained, as a reward for his patricide, the kingdom of Bengal. Sixteen

Ceylon

twin sons were born to him by an unusually fruitful Princess, of whom the eldest called Vijaya, after "many intolerable deeds of violence" was exiled from India and became the first King of Ceylon.

We now pass from the picturesque realms of the fairy story to history, since it is known that Vijaya arrived in the island about 500 B.C. and, landing on the north-west coast where Puttalam stands to-day, gradually subjugated the island. The King was a Brahmin, and he married a demon-worshipper who proved barren, and on his death c. 450 B.C., he was succeeded by his cousin Panduvasudeva, whose grandson, the great King Pandukabhaya, succeeded to the throne c. 400 B.C.

Pandukabhaya had a stormy youth, since it had been foretold that in the course of time he would murder ten maternal uncles, and in consequence the latter took natural and early measures to kill him first. Indeed, at the age of seven Pandukabhaya was bathing with some young friends in the jungle when his uncles' emissaries arrived to destroy him. But unlike his friends, who were naked, Panduka-bhaya was standing clothed on the bank, and diving into the pool he swam under water to the submerged hole of a hollow tree, where he hid. Meanwhile the emissaries counted the clothes on

The Mahawamsa, or the Greater Dynasty

the bank (probably each boy only possessed a *sarong* or cloth, as to-day), and killing one boy for every cloth they went their way, convinced that they had dispatched Pandukabhaya.

For the next ten years the boy lived in hiding, until one day he chanced to meet a learned Brahmin, who greeted him with the words: "Thou wilt be King, and full seventy years wilt thou rule; learn the art, my dear!" Besides advice, the Brahmin also supplied Pandukabhaya with the means to wage war against his uncles and dismissed him saying: "The woman at whose touch leaves turn to gold, make thou thy Queen, my dear." Much encouraged by this meeting, the Prince left to fight his maternal uncles, and on the way encountered, as was only right, a beautiful Princess called Pali "in a splendid waggon, bringing food to her father and the reapers." Pandukabhaya hastened to salute her, the Princess "stepped down from the waggon and, at the foot of a banyan-tree, she offered the Prince food in a golden bowl. Then she took banyan-leaves to entertain the rest of the people, and in an instant the leaves were changed into golden vessels." Naturally the Prince lost no time in making such a talented lady his wife.

Besides the protection of the Brahmin and the

Ceylon

magical powers of the lovely Pali, Pandukabhaya also obtained for his projected war the assistance of a most singular mare. This creature was indeed a "Yakkhini," or witch-mare, as her snow-white body and scarlet hooves might have implied. She was, moreover, little amenable to human control, as the Prince discovered when he first met her on the fringe of a pool near the Mahaweliganga River. "The Prince took a noose and came to capture her," we read in the Mahawamsa, "but when she saw him coming up behind her she fled for fear of his majestic aspect." Fortunately for Pandukabhaya, "she fled without rendering herself invisible," and eventually "he seized her by the mane and grasped a palm-leaf that was floating down the stream; by the effect of his merit this turned into a great sword." Then said the Prince: "I will slay thee!" But the witch-mare answered him: "I will conquer the kingdom and give it to thee, Lord! Slay me not!" So Pandukabhaya spared the "Yakkhini," although "he seized her by the neck and boring her nostrils with the point of his sword, he secured her thus with a rope." After this drastic treatment the humbled witch-mare "followed wheresoever he would."

With the acquisition of such spirited and unusual support the Prince then advanced to give

The Mahawamsa, or the Greater Dynasty

battle to his uncles, who awaited him in what is now the north central province. He was mounted, of course, on his "Yakkhini," who "neighed full loudly" when the "army raised a mighty battle-cry." The battle was decisive, since the Prince's forces killed all their opponents, including eight of the maternal uncles. After victory a mound of skulls was raised on the battlefield, with those of the uncles uppermost, and when Pandukabhaya inspected this macabre pyramid he remarked laconically: " 'Tis like a heap of gourds." Therefore his men called the neighbouring village "the village of the gourds," a name which it retains to this day.

But greater work than war awaited Pandukabhaya, since he was destined to become the founder of one of the most beautiful cities the world has ever known—Anuradhapura. The Mahawamsa records how after his great victory he proceeded to the palace of one of his surviving uncles who, with understandable alacrity, placed everything at the new King's disposal. Here Pandukabhaya decided to found his capital, and as a preliminary he ordered the state parasol of his uncle to be purified. This action signified his undisputed lordship, since the parasol, or *chatta*, even in such early times, was the symbol of sovereignty. The fact that the King's dispossessed

Ceylon

uncle was called Anuradha would appear the undoubted origin of the new city's name although, according to the Mahawamsa, it was founded under the constellation of Anuradha. The latter may be the original, or an additional, derivation. In any case, to Pandukabhaya fell the honour of being the first architect of Anuradhapura, although it was completely rebuilt in the course of the following centuries. The King laid out four suburbs, the Abhaya tank, the common cemetery, the place of execution, and many great temples. He also established the village boundaries throughout the whole of Ceylon. According to the Rajaviliya, Pandukabhaya built round Anuradhapura a rampart on which were carved figures of lions. Clearly this adventurous and romantic King had not forgotten his leonine origin. The Mahawamsa adds the further pleasing information: "Within the royal precincts he housed the 'Yakkhini' in the form of a mare." The chronicles say that Pandukabhaya died c. 300 B.C. at the age of one hundred and seven, having reigned for seventy years "in fair and wealthy Anuradhapura."

It was during the reign of his great-grandson, King Devanampiyatissa (247–207 B.C.), that the Buddhist religion was brought to Ceylon. This King, whose name means "Beloved of the Gods,"

The Mahawamsa, or the Greater Dynasty

was so pious that at the time of his consecration many wonders came to pass. Sapphires, beryls, and rubies rose of their own volition to the surface of the earth. The ocean as well desired to honour this exemplary monarch and, according to the Mahawamsa, "pearls of eight kinds, namely horse-pearl, elephant-pearl, waggon-pearl, myrobalan-pearl, bracelet-pearl, ring-pearl, kakudha fruit-pearl, and common pearls, came forth out of the sea and lay upon the shore in heaps."

Shortly after the beginning of King Devanampi-yatissa's reign his virtue and power became known to the Buddhist Emperor Asoka in India, who had recently succeeded to his throne after killing ninety-nine of his half-brothers, all of whom had been born of different mothers. That, however, did not prevent the Emperor, who was very devout, from deciding to convert Ceylon to Buddhism. In consequence he commissioned for this purpose his son Mahinda, who was a *thera*, or Buddhist monk. Mahinda must also have been a magician, since he passed through the air from India to the peak of a mountain near Anuradhapura which, after this inspiring flight, was known as Mihintale.

Meanwhile King Devanampiyatissa, "who had arranged a water-festival for the dwellers in the capital, set forth to enjoy the pleasures of the

Ceylon

chase," in the neighbourhood of this mountain. In the course of a hunt the quarry, in the form of an elk-stag, brought the King into the presence of Mahinda. Naturally the monarch was surprised to see the *thera*, and he could hardly believe his ears when the latter said, "Come hither, Tissa." However, convinced by this familiar form of address that the man was of a supernatural order, he approached him with deference and sat by his side. Such was the prelude to the conversion of King Devanampiyatissa and his whole kingdom to the Buddhist faith.

Before Mahinda left Ceylon, his mission accomplished, he promised the King that he would receive from India the right eye-tooth of the Lord Buddha together with his right collar-bone, his alms bowl, and later a branch from the sacred Bo-tree. The reception in the island of these precious relics is delightfully described in the Mahawamsa. On their arrival at Mihintale the excited monarch thought to himself: "If this is a relic of the Sage (Buddha), then shall my parasol bow down of itself, my elephant shall sink upon its knees, this relic-urn . . . shall descend upon my head. So thought the King, and as he thought so it came to pass. And as if sprinkled with ambrosia, the King was full of joy and, taking the

The Mahawamsa, or the Greater Dynasty

urn from his head, he set it on the back of an elephant. Then did the elephant trumpet joyfully and the earth quaked." When the relics were about to be enshrined in the Thuparama at Anuradhapura the urn rose up in the air from the elephant's back, and once more rested on the delighted monarch's head.

The arrival in Ceylon of the branch of the Bo-tree from Buddha Gaya was heralded by many miracles. A gold vase was made to receive it measuring nine cubits in circumference, "having the upper edge the size of a young elephant's trunk, and being in radiancy equal to the young morning sun." When the vase was placed in the vicinity of the Bo-tree an active branch miraculously detached itself from the trunk and embedded itself in the earth contained in the golden vase. During the voyage from India lotus flowers of five different colours blossomed round the ship and "manifold instruments of music resounded in the air." On arrival in Ceylon, King Devanampiyatissa descended neck-deep into the water to receive the vase and bestowed upon the Bo-tree the Kingship of Lanka. It was then brought in state to Anuradhapura, where it exists to-day, being nearly two thousand two hundred years old.

The acceptance of Buddhism caused a great

Ceylon

spiritual ferment in Ceylon, and as a result the first great religious buildings were erected in Anuradhapura by orders of the King. This architectural efflorescence continued for about fifty years after the death of Devanampiyatissa in 207 B.C., but in 145 B.C. a Tamil from southern India, named Elara, conquered the greater part of the island and held it for nearly half a century. Although a Hindu, and therefore indifferent to the beauties of Anuradhapura, King Elara was a just if impetuous monarch. The Mahawamsa records that "at the head of his bed he had a bell hung up with a long rope, so that those who desired a judgment at law might ring it." One night the King was disturbed by an intelligent cow "dragging at the bell in bitterness of heart," as her calf had been killed by the chariot of the King's son. Elara immediately caused the Prince's head to be severed from his body by the wheel of the same chariot. On another occasion a broken-hearted hen, whose chicken had been devoured by a snake, pulled the bell and related to the monarch her tragedy. Elara at once had the erring reptile brought before him, and the chicken, fortunately still alive, was cut out of the snake's quivering body, which was then hung upon a tree as a warning to other voracious cobras.

The Mahawamsa, or the Greater Dynasty

While King Elara was thus engaged in dispensing justice to man and beast the exiled Singalese royalties, living in the hill country at Rohuna, were planning to regain the throne. King Kakavannatissa, the grandson of Devanampiyatissa, was now the head of the family, and he possessed a very determined wife in Queen Viharadevi. This lady harboured three very peculiar desires, since, according to the Mahawamsa, she wished "to eat the honey that remained when she had given twelve thousand *bhikkhus* to eat of it; and then she longed to drink the water that had served to cleanse the sword with which the head of the first warrior among King Elara's warriors had been struck off, and to drink that water standing on his very head." The Queen's third wish was less masochistic, since she only desired "to adorn herself with garlands of unfaded lotus blossoms from the lotus marshes of Anuradhapura."

When King Kakavannatissa was informed of his wife's singular inclinations he decided that their cause was pregnancy, and that therefore it was the more urgent that they should be gratified. So his agents contrived to bring back to Rohuna the head of one of Elara's warriors and garlands of lotus blooms from Anuradhapura, and in due time Queen Viharadevi gave birth to a son called

Ceylon

Gamani, and two years later to another boy she named Tissa. These two young men were destined to exercise great influence on the future of Ceylon.

At an early age Prince Gamani showed courage and skill in "guiding elephants and horses, and in bearing the sword," and he was by no means content with the restricted patrimony held by his father Kakavannatissa. Thrice he asked the King for permission to fight Elara and his Tamils, and each time it was refused. Then most disrespectfully Gamani sent his father a woman's garment with the message: "If my father were a man, he would not speak thus: therefore shall he put this on." So incensed was the King by this insolent behaviour that the Prince was forced to take refuge in Malay, while the Singalese nicknamed him "Duttha," or angry Gamani.

Towards the close of the second century before Christ, King Kakavannatissa died and, Dutthagamani being abroad, Queen Viharavedi and her younger son Tissa usurped the elder Prince's slender inheritance. But Dutthagamani hearing of this returned to Rohuna, defeated his brother in battle, and after forgiving his treachery he enlisted the support of Prince Tissa on his side. Then the rightful King of Lanka, Dutthagamani, collected

The Mahawamsa, or the Greater Dynasty

his forces, and descending into the plains advanced against Elara at Anuradhapura.

As the Buddha had been assisted by his horse Kanthaka and King Pandukabhaya by his witch-mare the "Yakkhini," so was King Dutthagamani aided to victory by his elephant Kandula, who was "foremost in strength, beauty, shape, and in the qualities of courage and swiftness and in mighty size." This great beast bore the King to Wijito on the road to Anuradhapura, and arriving outside the city they found it was defended with a high wall, furnished with gates of wrought iron. Undeterred by this obstacle and "placing himself upon his knees, and battering stones, mortar and bricks with his tusks, did the elephant attack the gate of iron." In reply the Tamils dropped molten pitch on to his back, which so tormented Kandula that he "betook him to a pool of water and dived there . . . then did the best of beasts again proudly take heart, and trumpeting he reared himself out of the water and stood defiantly on firm land." Then "after the elephant's physician had washed the pitch away and put on balm, the King mounted the elephant, and stroking his temples with his hand he cheered him on with the words: 'To thee I give, dear Kandula, the lordship over the whole island of Lanka.'"

Ceylon

Stimulated by this honour the noble animal returned to battle with a seven times folded buffalo hide, steeped in oil, under his armour. "Roaring like thunder he came . . . and with his tusks pierced the panels of the gate . . . and with uproar the gate crashed to the ground." Kandula must have presented a terrifying spectacle to the Tamils as he entered Wijito brandishing a cart-wheel in his trunk. After capturing the town Dutthagamani advanced on Anuradhapura. Outside this city another fierce struggle took place, in which Kandula of course was most actively engaged. The main body of the Tamils, with Elara in their midst, was defeated after a stubborn fight, and Dutthagamani pursued his opponent to the south gate of Anuradhapura, proclaiming: "None but myself shall slay Elara." Outside the gate a homeric battle was raged by the two Kings. Elara first hurled his javelin, but Dutthagamani evaded it. Then Kandula charged, rending the body of the rival elephant with his tusks, while Dutthagamani closed with Elara and killed him with his dagger.

Thus ended an epic struggle by which the victor united Lanka under his rule, and the King, being of a generous disposition, commanded that on the spot where Elara had fallen a monument should be erected to his memory. Ever after the Kings of

The Mahawamsa, or the Greater Dynasty

Ceylon, when passing this place, alighted to pay their respects to a brave enemy, and as late as 1818, after an unsuccessful rebellion against British rule, the defeated leader got down from his litter and walked past the traditional locality of Elara's death.

The Mahawamsa records how Dutthagamani celebrated his great victory and his humanitarian reflections on this occasion. "Sitting then on the terrace of the Royal Palace, adorned, lighted with fragrant lamps and filled with many a perfume, magnificent with nymphs in the guise of dancing-girls, while he rested on his soft and fair couch, covered with costly draperies, he, looking back upon his glorious victory, great though it was, knew no joy, remembering that thereby was wrought the destruction of millions of beings."

King Dutthagamani was the most illustrious sovereign of the greater dynasty, being a great warrior, a beneficent ruler, and the principal architect of Anuradhapura. He died in 77 B.C. after a reign of twenty-four years, surrounded on his death-bed, according to the Mahawamsa, by ninety-six thousand *bhikkhus*, who had come to pay their last tribute to this most priest-ridden of kings. His heir was his brother Tissa, and turning to him he said: "Evening and morning offer thou

Ceylon

flowers at the Great Thupa (which enshrined Buddha's collar-bone). . . . Never grow weary, my dear, in duty towards the brotherhood." At that moment there arrived six supernatural chariots, and into one of them the King was reborn in celestial form and, like Elijah, was taken up into Heaven.

King Tissa, who succeeded, carried on the great building schemes in Anuradhapura, but thirty years later the Tamils captured the city and five kings of that race ruled from 44 to 27 B.C. In the latter year Vatthagamani reconquered the Singalese throne, and his son Coranga was reigning at the beginning of the Christian era. The wife of this King Queen Anula succeeded, by her desperate deeds, in bestowing some renown on this obscure period of Singalese history, since in the course of seven years she murdered six monarchs, five of whom were her husbands. Enamoured of one of the palace guards, called Siva, Anula poisoned Coranga and also his successor Tissa, and made Siva King of Lanka. But after a year and two months the Queen tired of Siva, and finding Vatuka, a carpenter, who pleased her, she poisoned Siva and made Vatuka king. The latter also held Anula's affections for a year and two months, when he in his turn was murdered to make way

The Mahawamsa, or the Greater Dynasty

for a sturdy woodsman called Tissa. This King, less fortunate than his two immediate predecessors, only reigned for a year and one month, when the Queen poisoned him in order to raise to the throne the Brahmin Niliya, a palace priest. Despite this more respectable choice of a husband, the Mahawamsa relates: "When the Princess Anula (who desired to take her pleasure, even as she listed, with thirty-two of the palace guards) had put to death Niliya also with poison, the Queen Anula herself reigned four months." It is with some natural gratification that one learns that, after this brief period of sole rule, the infamous Anula was put to death by Kutakannatissa, the nephew of her first victim Coranga. This King reigned for twenty-two years, and was succeeded by Bhatikabhaya in A.D. 38.

This virtuous and intelligent King managed, during a thirty years' reign, to efface the evil memory of Queen Anula by his just and enlightened government. He had, moreover, a profound belief in the power of flowers to mitigate the brutality of human passions and to increase the spiritual well-being of his subjects. Thus the Mahawamsa records: "When the King had commanded that the Great Cetiya of Ruanweli, from the Vedika (altar) at the foot to the parasol at the

Ceylon

top, be plastered with a paste of sweet-smelling unguent, four fingers thick, and that flowers be carefully embedded therein by their stalks, he made the thupa even as a globe of flowers." Those who are familiar with the size of Ruanweli and the beauty of the flowers of Ceylon can perhaps visualize the exquisite nature of the floral offerings of King Bhatikabhaya.

The following two hundred years of Ceylonese history were occupied by two groups of rulers called respectively the "Twelve" and the "Thirteen Kings." They were all Singalese monarchs, mostly of the House of Vijaya; several were murdered, and the majority were compelled to propitiate the ever-growing power of the *bhikkhus*. Lanka at this period was a truly "priest-ridden" state, but there is no indication in the chronicles of the period that the exaltation of the *bhikkhus* was resented by the people. In A.D. 325 King Mahasena succeeded to the throne and proved himself to be a monarch of more character than his predecessors. He even dared to oppose the majority of the priests by supporting a heretical minority, and he pulled down the "Brazen Palace" in Anuradhapura, which was the principal centre of orthodoxy in the state. But as an older man Mahasena became more indulgent towards the orthodox *bhikkhus* and, before

The Sulawamsa, or the Lesser Dynasty

he died in A.D. 352, he had built on their behalf the beautiful Jetavanarama Dagoba at Anuradhapura and the great tanks of Mineriya and Kantalai. These works bear evidence to-day to this fertile conversion of King Mahasena.

(b) *The Sulawamsa*

Besides being the keen architect of edifices and reservoirs, Mahasena had also the privilege of being the last King of the Mahawamsa, or Greater Dynasty. He was followed by the Kings of the Sulawamsa, or Lesser Dynasty, who, it must be noted, were inferior in power and not in race, since the first monarch of the latter dynasty was the son of Mahasena. Nevertheless, with the Sulawamsa began a diminution of the King's abilities to withstand the Tamil invasions, which swiftly led to that loss of wealth and independence from which Ceylon has never recovered. The Rajaviliya laments and explains this decline of royal authority by saying that the kings of the Sulawamsa were "no longer of unmixed blood, but the offspring of parents, only one of whom was descended from the Sun."

With such a deplorable ancestry, it was perhaps only natural that of the sixty-two kings who ruled

Ceylon

from A.D. 352 to 1100 four committed suicide, one was killed by the Tamils, two died in exile, and nine were murdered by close relations. There were, however, some enlightened and even endearing monarchs in the early Sulawamsa. Mahasena's younger son, King Detutissa, was a skilled sculptor and, according to the Rajaviliya, he made "with his own hands images, from pieces of ivory, sandalwood and stone," of the Buddha for the edification of his more pious subjects. His son, King Buddhadaasa, was an expert surgeon and a thoughtful man, since he appointed "a leech, an astrologer, and a learned Buddhist priest in each village of the island of Lanka." Some years later King Kumavadasen entertained such a lively affection both for the work and person of the poet Kalidassa that, on the latter's death, this monarch immolated himself on the funeral pyre. But the devout or altruistic actions of individual kings could not stem the tide of Tamil incursions, nor the declining prosperity of Ceylon.

There was, however, a brief interlude in this long history of ineffectual monarchs, when about A.D. 450 Prince Dhatu Sena, discarding the orange robes of a *bhikkhu*, drove out the Tamils, who had dominated Ceylon for the last twenty-five years. But the story of King Dhatu Sena and his patricide

The Sulawamsa, or the Lesser Dynasty

son Kasyapa is so firmly linked with Sigiriya that the mention of his reign must be postponed to the chapter on that subject. Early in the sixth century the Tamils returned to the island in great force and controlled the north of Ceylon for nearly five hundred years. Indeed, during the eighth century the Singalese found it impossible to hold Anuradhapura any longer, and that magnificent city, the home of five million people and of countless treasures of art, was occupied and pillaged by the Tamils. In the same century King Kuda Akbo began the erection of Polonnaruwa and made it the capital of Singalese Ceylon, but his successors only held it until A.D. 1000, when it suffered at the hands of the Tamils the same fate as Anuradhapura. The year 1065 (it almost coincided with a remarkable event in England) witnessed a revival of fortune for the Singalese monarchy when Vijaya Bahu I emerged from the recesses of Rohuna, overthrew the Tamils, and having captured Polonnaruwa was crowned King of all Lanka at Anuradhapura. But his famous grandson, King Parakrama Bahu I, outshone all these notable exploits, and the story of his thirty years' reign deserves the detailed consideration befitting the last King of Lanka who was worthy of that illustrious heritage.

Ceylon

Early in life Parakrama disposed of some obstacles on his path to the throne in the form of superfluous uncles and cousins, and in A.D. 1155 he was crowned King at Anuradhapura. Parakrama, who was "lotus-faced" and had "eyes that were long like the lily," was a great statesman and an enlightened man. He was also a great warrior since, not content with crushing the Tamils in Ceylon, he collected an army of over two million men and, transporting them to southern India, he subjugated the King of Pandy and compelled him to pay tribute to Ceylon for the rest of his reign. On his return Parakrama rebuilt the great city of Polonnaruwa with the aid of Hindu artists he had brought back from India. This accounts for so many buildings in Polonnaruwa being in the "Dravidian" style of architecture. Some authorities even suggest that the King himself was a Hindu rather than a Buddhist, and there is no doubt that his impartiality towards both religions was directly responsible for the corruption of the ethics of Buddhism by the primitive worship of the Hindu gods.

Besides the existing buildings at Polonnaruwa described in the next chapter, Parakrama erected a chain of ramparts around the city, a theatre for dance and song and "a charming palace, supported

The Sulawamsa, or the Lesser Dynasty

on one column, which seemed to have sprung up, as it were, by the bursting of the earth. Its floor of gold was lighted only by one chandelier." He also restored the three great dagobas at Anuradhapura, which for long had been covered with undergrowth "where lurked tigers and bears," and there he "caused the monks to be seated and gave them much alms." He also forbade that "animals in the whole of Lanka, both of the earth and of the water, should be killed." Above all, he established such peace and security in Ceylon that "even a woman might traverse the island with a precious jewel, and not be asked what it was."

King Parakrama Bahu was solaced during his reign by two wives of outstanding virtue and intelligence. The one he loved the more was Queen Rupavati, who was an expert musician and dancer. Her beauty also must have been phenomenal, since "she drew upon her the eyes of the world," and her chastity was no less renowned, for "save her own husband, she regarded not, as much even as a blade of grass, any other person." In this the Queen was prudent as well as virtuous, since in the course of the centuries the Kings of Lanka had devised some exquisite tortures for unfaithful wives. Parakrama's second Queen of note was Leelavati, famous for her learning as well as for

Ceylon

the comeliness of her person. She was responsible for the erection of a large palace to house the manuscripts she had collected, and to-day there stands at Polonnaruwa the great statue of Parakrama Bahu facing, across an expanse of jungle, the ruined library built by that erudite Queen.

King Parakrama Bahu I died in A.D. 1186, and the Rajaviliya tells us that his spiritual form was located "on a silver rock in the wilderness of the Himalayas, where are eighty-four mountains of gold, and where he will reign as King as long as the world endures."

After the death of this illustrious monarch the history of Ceylon is melancholy to study. Weak and selfish kings succeeded each other, while the Tamil invasions increased in power and number. Polonnaruwa was abandoned about 1300, Yapahuwa which succeeded it as the capital a hundred years later when Cotta, near Colombo, became the residence of the King. In 1592, however, Kandy became the capital of the Kingdom of Lanka, and retained that position until its final eclipse at the beginning of the nineteenth century. The fifteenth century, however, was important in the history of Ceylon owing to the strong, if ephemeral, connection with China at that time.

The first Chinaman to visit the island was, as

The Sulawamsa, or the Lesser Dynasty

mentioned in the Introduction, Fa-Hien about the year A.D. 400, and a little later a Singalese mission went to Pekin bearing a superb jade image of the Buddha for the Emperor. A common religion and mutual trading arrangements maintained the connection between the two countries through the centuries, until in 1410 General Ching-Ho arrived in Ceylon at the head of a large army, with the avowed purpose of impressing Vijaya Bahu IV with the power of China. The King, however, received the Chinese as enemies, and his attempt to plunder the mission led to his defeat and capture by Ching-Ho. He then suffered the further humiliation of being taken as a prisoner to Pekin, where he was formally deposed by the Emperor, who elevated to the throne his son, Parakrama Bahu VI. Thereafter the power of the Chinese gradually waned in Ceylon, although until the end of the fifteenth century tribute was paid twice annually to the Emperor, and on two occasions this was taken to Pekin by the Singalese kings themselves. By 1500 intercourse between the two countries had been finally severed, and to-day the itinerant Chinese merchant with a large pile of silk fabrics on the back of his bicycle remains the only link between Ceylon and China. The effect which a permanent domination of Ceylon by the Chinese

Ceylon

might have had on the future of the East remains one of the fascinating "Ifs" of history.

Hardly had the Singalese been disembarrassed of their Chinese visitors, when in 1522 startling news was brought by a messenger to King Dhamma Parakrama Bahu at his capital of Cotta. According to the Rajaviliya, the man reported that "there is in our harbour of Colombo a race of people fair of skin and comely withal. They don jackets of iron and hats of iron: they rest not a minute in one place." Together with this restiveness, so astonishing to the phlegmatic Singalese, "they eat hunks of white stone and drink blood," the messenger said, "and they have guns with a noise louder than thunder, and a ball shot from one of them, after traversing a league, will break a castle of marble."

What had actually happened to the unfortunate Singalese was that the first of three European invasions of Ceylon had begun. Fortuitously, since their ships had been driven into Colombo by a strong current, the Portuguese had arrived in the island. The King was naturally incredulous that such a strange people could exist, and he therefore sent his son in disguise to Colombo in order to discover the truth. The Prince on his return said to his father: "To fight these men is useless; it

The Sulawamsa, or the Lesser Dynasty

will be well to give them audience." The King agreed, the Portuguese came to Cotta, presents were exchanged, and at once they began their subtle encroachments on the Kingdom of Lanka. Sometimes supporting the Sovereign in his interminable struggles with his own people, at others assisting those in revolt against the King, the Portuguese succeeded in the course of fifty years in subjugating all those parts of the coast and mainland which were valuable for trading cinnamon and other spices to different parts of the East. These spices, first used entirely for preserving and only later for flavouring food, comprised at that time, and indeed until the nineteenth century, the main export trade of Ceylon.

It is important at this point to understand the attitude of the Portuguese towards their new subjects, since it was entirely different to that of either of their successors, the Dutch or the English. Throughout the latter Middle Ages the Portuguese were crusaders and explorers before they were merchants. Consequently their primary aim in their new territories was to convert the inhabitants to the Catholic Church, and their second was to add the fruits of their exploration to the Kingdom of Portugal. The latter they achieved until the middle of the seventeenth century, but their

Ceylon

attempts to convert the Singalese kings to Christianity bore likewise no permanent results, although many under Portuguese rule accepted it, in particular along the coast. The sincerity of their convictions is proved to-day by their successors, since nearly all the fisherfolk belong to the Roman Catholic Church.

The first religious success won by the Portuguese was in 1530, when King Bhuvaneka Bahu allowed his heir, Prince Dharmapala, to be baptized a Christian with the name of Juan. He even sent to Lisbon, as a proof of his sincerity, a statue of the boy cast in gold with a jewelled crown. This statue was taken in procession to the Cathedral, where a strange coronation was enacted by King John III of Portugal. In 1542 this Prince became King Don Juan Dharmapala Bahu, the first Christian sovereign of Ceylon, although his rule only extended to those parts of the island held by the Portuguese. On his death in 1582 a member of the royal family, called for his prowess Raja Sinha, or the "Lion-King," proclaimed himself sovereign of the whole of Ceylon, deposed the rightful heir, Jaya-Weira, and rallied the country against the Portuguese. Nevertheless, despite several victories he was unable to conquer Colombo, although he besieged it on two occasions, once with a force

The Sulawamsa, or the Lesser Dynasty

of fifty thousand warriors and two thousand elephants.

On Raja Sinha's death in 1592, at the advanced age of a hundred and twenty, another royal Christian with the name of Don Juan secured the throne. Having been assisted by the Portuguese, he soon repudiated them and abandoned Christianity. He then reverted to his original name of Wimala Dhamma and, leaving Cotta, became the first King of Kandy. After these initial successes the new King greatly strengthened his position by a great victory over the Portuguese, by which he secured and married the rightful claimant to the throne, the Catholic Donna Catharina, who was the heiress of Jaya-Weira, deposed by Raja Sinha in 1582. His victory, however, was marred by the grossest cruelty, since, according to the Rajaviliya, "he put out the eyes of the Portuguese whom he had taken, cut off their ears, and leaving only one eye for each of five men sent them down to Colombo, holding one another by the hand." On the death of Wimala Dhamma in 1604, Donna Catharina became the undisputed heiress to the throne, and although she married her brother-in-law Senarat, who was a Buddhist, Portuguese influence in Ceylon was then at its height. St. Francis Xavier, the great missionary, was in the

Ceylon

island at that time, and the number of converts, together with the military and mercantile pre-eminence of the Portuguese, gave the impression that Catholicism might soon supplant Buddhism as the national religion of Ceylon.

The initial frustration of these hopes dated from the reign of Wimala Dhamma, who in 1602 invited the assistance of the Dutch in his war against the Portuguese, and two years later the former succeeded in building a fort at Cottiar near Trincomalee. This primary achievement the Dutch were unable to develop for the time being, since both Donna Catharina, who died in 1617, and King Senarat, who ruled for a further fifteen years, were only concerned in using the Dutch as a foil to the Portuguese. But when their son Raja Sinha II succeeded in 1632 he made a definite alliance with the Dutch with the object of driving the Portuguese out of Ceylon. It would be superfluous in these pages to trace the fluctuations of fortune experienced by these two protagonists during the first half of the seventeenth century. The Portuguese stubbornly resisted the increasing aggression of the Dutch and, but for the assistance of Raja Sinha, it is improbable that the Dutch would have won the war. Colombo finally capitulated in 1658, and the Portuguese commander

The Sulawamsa, or the Lesser Dynasty

withdrew to Goa, leaving all his country's possessions in Ceylon to be absorbed by the Dutch.

It is important to distinguish between the different natures of these two European dominations in Ceylon. The Portuguese, as has been said, were primarily missionaries and conquerors, and in their dealings with the Singalese treated them as a subject people. The activities of the Dutch, on the other hand, were essentially concentrated on commerce, and in order to obtain better terms for their merchants they were prepared to endure offensive and even barbarous treatment. The massacre or mutilation of a few individuals had to be disregarded for the general benefit of their mercenary nation. As regards religion, the Dutch persecuted the Catholic Singalese relentlessly, with the primary object of eradicating Portuguese influence, although naturally their Calvinistic beliefs must have increased their pleasure in destroying the work of the Catholic missions. But, unlike the Portuguese, the practice of commerce left the Dutch little time to convert the Singalese to Calvinism, so that to-day, when Ceylon is governed by a race which is neither Catholic nor Calvinistic, there are only nine conventicles belonging to the Dutch Reformed Faith, while the Roman Catholic

Ceylon

religion is practised in over eight hundred churches in the island.

The Dutch domination of the lowlands, although commercial in purpose, was founded on force, like that of the Portuguese; and Raja Sinha II, who was so largely responsible for the Dutch victory, soon discovered that the resources of his kingdom were being as harshly exploited by the Dutch as they had been by the Portuguese. This king was a remarkable if unamiable figure, and fortunately there is a picturesque account of his character and reign in *The Historical Relation of Ceylon* written by the sailor, Robert Knox, who was his prisoner from 1660 to 1680, having been captured near Trincomalee, where his ship had put in for repairs. Although Knox was treated with humanity by the King, he has some astonishing stories to tell of this monarch's behaviour to his own subjects.

Raja Sinha II in his autocracy and brutalities was typical of the Kings of the Sulawamsa, who had lost the vision and great ability of the Kings of the Mahawamsa. In appearance this ruler was a striking figure since, according to Knox, although he was not tall, he was "well set with great rolling eyes, a brisk bold look, a great swelling belly, and very lively in his actions and behaviour; in conclusion a very comely man." His dress was most exotic

The Sulawamsa, or the Lesser Dynasty

and borrowed from many sources. He wore Moorish pantaloons, a Portuguese doublet, and on his head "a cap with four corners like a Jesuit's, three tiers high, and a feather standing upright before, like that in the head of a fore-horse in a team." Despite Knox's simile, it would seem improbable that any member of the Society of Jesus has ever worn such a flamboyant hat.

In character Raja Sinha was sober, calculating, and cruel. Knox writes, "as he is abstemious in his eating, so in the use of women. If he useth them 'tis unknown and with great secrecy. He hath not had the company of his queen for twenty years." One lapse, however, is recorded by Knox. "He had a daughter that was with child by himself; but in childbed both died." His cruelty towards his attendants was particularly sinister. Most of these were boys and, according to Knox, "comely and of good descent," and he adds: "these boys go bare-headed with long hair hanging down their backs." It would appear that they were taken by force from their parents for Raja Sinha's use, and while the boys served the King the parents were free from all taxation. Nevertheless, after a short time in his service, during which "no women are admitted, be it his mother that bare him," each boy was inevitably murdered. The King "requiteth

Ceylon

them," writes Knox, "by cutting off their heads, and putting them into their bellies." After these painful details Knox hastens to assure his readers that the King had no homosexual tendencies.

Raja Sinha relied on the chastening effect of public torture and execution to retain his power over his subjects. He had indeed a variety of punishments for those who displeased him. Some had their flesh pulled off by pincers, others had hot irons clamped to the more tender parts of their bodies, while their severed hands were hung round their necks. Sometimes, according to Knox, the King commanded "to make them eat their own flesh, and their own mothers to eat of their own children; and so to lead them through the city to terrify all, unto the place of execution, the dogs following to eat them. For they are so accustomed to it, that seeing a prisoner led away, follow after."

More amiable in character were the King's hobbies, sports, and athletic exercises. Besides keeping a large collection of tame deer and leopard and "strange kinds of beasts and birds," Raja Sinha was an excellent shot with a gun inlaid with gold, silver, and ivory. He also possessed nine cannons captured from the Dutch, which he much prized. These were "all rarely carved, and inlayed with

The Sulawamsa, or the Lesser Dynasty

silver and brass and coloured stones, set in convenient places, and painted with images and flowers." When in his palace at Kandy, Knox reports that he "passeth his time with looking upon certain Toys and Fancies that he hath." But Raja Sinha's favourite simple pleasure was aquatic. "He takes great delight in swimming," writes Knox, "in which he is very expert. And the custom is, when he goeth into the water, that all his attendance that can swim must go in likewise." It may safely be assumed that little "attendance" remained on the bank.

As a ruler Raja Sinha II was an undoubted success. During a reign of fifty-five years he was only embarrassed by one rebellion, and to ensure himself against another outbreak he poisoned his only son. His attitude towards foreigners was crafty and cynical. After this rebellion, for instance, the King sent down the leader to Colombo in the hope that the Dutch "would invent new tortures for him, beyond what he knew of." But the Dutch relieved the man of his chains and retained him in the expectation of using him later against the King. Raja Sinha made continual efforts to alienate both individual Portuguese and Dutch from their respective loyalties, since their knowledge was useful to him in military and adminis-

Ceylon

trative affairs. After the surrender of Colombo to the Dutch, for example, the King invited any Portuguese who so desired to come to Kandy. Many accepted, and found with Raja Sinha not only employment, but also an occasional opportunity to practise their religion, which was impossible under the Dutch. Knox tells a story about the King and a Jesuit priest worthy of repetition here. He sent for a certain Father Vergonce, whose life had been spent in attending to the spiritual needs of the Singalese Catholics, and asked him to "lay aside his old coat and cap" and receive honour and wealth from the King. But the old priest replied that "he boasted more in that old habit and in the Name of Jesus than in all the honour he could do him." This fine reply pleased Raja Sinha, and Father Vergonce was allowed to end his days in peace.

The King's partiality for Europeans was founded not only on his belief in their superior capabilities, but also on a certain superstition prevalent amongst the Singalese. According to Knox, it was generally believed that European "Gods are white, and that the souls of the Blessed after the Resurrection shall be white; and therefore that black is a rejected and accursed colour." Raja Sinha II died in 1687 at the approximate age of ninety, and in

The Sulawamsa, or the Lesser Dynasty

assessing the character and achievements of this remarkable man it should be realized that his cruelties were in accordance with the practice of his age and country, while by his personal renown and ability in dealing with the Dutch and the Portuguese he gave his people half a century of comparative peace and prosperity.

After the death of this king the power of his successors diminished, and in consequence the Dutch were enabled to strengthen their commercial stranglehold on the island. In 1739 the royal line became extinct and a Malabar secured the throne of Lanka. A determined but unsuccessful rebellion against the Dutch broke out in 1766, and sixteen years later the Singalese, who had already suffered from the predatory instincts of Tamils, Chinese, Portuguese, and Dutch, were faced by the incursion of a new enemy in an armed force from the British Empire.

The connection between England and Ceylon up to that time had been slight. In 1579 Queen Elizabeth had indeed sent one of her useful privateers "to cruize upon the Portuguese," and H.M.S. *Edward Bonaventure* had made an unsuccessful attempt to sack the prosperous town of Galle. Ten years later a certain Mr. Ralph Fitch from India was the first known Englishman to visit

Ceylon

Ceylon, and in the following century Mr. Knox, as already related, was compelled to spend twenty years in the island. But the English Government remained uninterested in Ceylon until the eighteenth century when, with the development of British rule in India, the necessity of occupying Ceylon was the cause of Sir Hector Munro's seizure of Trincomalee in 1782. England was then at war with Holland, but little progress was made against the Dutch until 1795. In that year Holland was overrun by the armies of the French Republic, and she was naturally unable to support her isolated forces in Ceylon. England instantly took advantage of this welcome enfeeblement of her old rival, and by the use of force and intrigue she had secured all the Dutch possessions in the island by 1796. Few British conquests have been made at the cost of so little blood and money.

At first the English conquests in Ceylon were administered by the Governor of Madras in the interests of the British East India Company, and an official of the name of Andrews was authorized by the Company to collect the taxes. Unfortunately Mr. Andrews, either through necessity or ineptitude, farmed out these taxes to the Moors and Parsees on the coast, and owing to this inequitable system of taxation there was a general rising of

The Sulawamsa, or the Lesser Dynasty

the Singalese under the British rule in 1797. This insurrection was easily suppressed; nevertheless, Mr. Pitt transferred the English possessions in Ceylon to the Crown, appointing as governor the Hon. Frederick North, later Lord Guilford, who gained instant popularity by his more humane methods of taxation.

Up to that time the British had not dealt with the King of Kandy, except in so far as their trading interests were concerned. But Mr. North received instructions to extend the sphere of British interests, and he therefore initiated secret conversations with the Adigar, or chief minister, of King Wikrema Raja Sinha. The main object of this manœuvre, which reflected little credit on Mr. North's integrity, was to incite the King to senseless acts of cruelty in order to dishonour him in Singalese eyes, and also to urge him to an act of aggression which could give the English an excuse to seize the kingdom of Kandy.

At first these intrigues were eminently successful. Sri Wikrema Raja Sinha required little encouragement to persecute his subjects, and early in 1803, exasperated by the alternate threats and cajoleries of Mr. North and the Adigar, the King committed the desired act of aggression against some English property. War was at once declared,

Ceylon

and General McDowell occupied Kandy with three thousand men, the King escaping to the mountains. The general then signed an advantageous treaty with the Adigar, who now ruled in place of the King, and withdrew from Kandy, leaving there only a small garrison to implement their agreement.

Mr. North did not long enjoy the fruits of this Machiavellian victory, since on June 24, 1803, the Adigar massacred the English troops in Kandy and restored Sri Wikrema Raja Sinha to the throne. The exigencies of the Napoleonic wars prevented the British from revenging this outrage for a time, and it is pleasant to know that during the following twelve years the King succeeded in retaining his throne, he disembarrassed him, by execution, of the treacherous Adigar. In 1815, however, Sri Wikrema Raja Sinha committed a less prudent action by seizing some English merchants, and, cutting off their hands, ears and noses, he tied these members round their necks and drove them into Colombo. The British, having recently vanquished Bonaparte, now felt encouraged to encompass the downfall of the King of Kandy. A large force was therefore collected, and in March 1815 Kandy was occupied, the King deposed, and the chiefs signed a convention with the English governor which, while vesting Ceylon in the

The Sulawamsa, or the Lesser Dynasty

British Crown, guaranteed to the Singalese their ancient privileges and the free practice of their religion.

The English celebrated their final victory in Ceylon by an action which was creditable to their humanity but incomprehensible to the Singalese. The state elephants, whose main occupation had been the methodical dismemberment of human beings, were turned loose into the jungle. But these intelligent animals soon gave proof of their traditional memories by returning regularly to Kandy at those seasons during which they had been called on to exercise their profession of executioners. The English authorities were considerably shocked by this bestial precocity and much relieved when, after a few years, these sadistic mammals accepted the inevitable and remained in the jungle.

Sri Wikrema Raja Sinha, who was the last King of a dynasty which had ruled in Ceylon for over two thousand three hundred years, appears to have presented that prosperous appearance usually associated with a mid-Victorian member of a London club. According to a contemporary, he was five foot nine inches in height, "slightly corpulent, stoutly made and muscular. He had a pleasant expression of countenance, a handsome beard,

Ceylon

broad shoulders and a full chest." When the King was deposed and taken to Colombo in 1815 he must have retained this pleasant expression, since on being shown his prison quarters he remarked, "As I am no longer permitted to be King, I am thankful for all the kindness and attention which has been shown to me." It was also, no doubt, a well-deserved compliment to the British authorities. Later the King was exiled to India.

With the deposition of Sri Wikrema Raja Sinha the native monarchy was finally extinguished in Ceylon, but despite the traditional extortions, cruelty, and ineptitude of their kings, the Singalese accepted with neither gratitude nor meekness the British rule. A serious but unsuccessful revolt broke out in 1817, and the "Year of Revolution," 1848, had its distant but resonant echo in Ceylon, where the people of Kandy, led by the *bhikkhus*, again rebelled. In the great rock temple at Dambulla a young man was crowned King of Lanka; but the governor, Lord Torrington, crushed with little difficulty these premature hopes of liberty. Gradually and without violence similar aspirations are being realized to-day.

Chapter Five

THE LOST CITIES

☼

(a) *The Dagoba*

To appreciate fully the "Lost Cities," it is essential to realize that they were ecclesiastical rather than civic in foundation and atmosphere. No medieval town in Europe was more dependent on the Church than were the Singalese cities on Buddhism. Both kings and nobles rejoiced in their subserviency to the *bhikkhus*, and royal and aristocratic piety were alone judged on this ingenuous criterion. In consequence, the principal edifices in every city were of an ecclesiastical order, and of these by far the most important were the dagobas which, owing to their solid construction, remain to-day the chief architectural features of the "Lost Cities." The origin, function, and appearance of the dagoba must therefore receive brief consideration.

These vast erections of brick and stucco, which so amaze the visitor to-day, had a humble origin. They are derived from the primitive tumuli, or *stupas*, for the burial of the dead, which existed in

Ceylon

Ceylon long before the advent of Buddhism. When, however, King Devanampiyatissa received from the Emperor Asoka the alms bowl and collar-bone of the Buddha, amongst other sacred relics, it was clearly necessary to build more imposing edifices to house them than the insignificant tumuli. In consequence, the tumulus developed into a large hemispherical brick dome, enshrining the relic-chamber, which was crowned by a square block of brickwork, called the *tee*, containing offerings, while surmounting the whole rose one or more representations of an umbrella, the symbol of royal power in the East. Thus shortly was evolved the dagoba, a name derived from the two words "Datu," meaning a relic, and "Gabbhan" a shrine.

There are a few further considerations which may help the traveller in his appreciation of these magnificent erections. The umbrella above the *tee* became stylized, in the course of time, into the conical spire which is most common to-day. All important dagobas were, and often still are, provided with railings called "Vedikas" which, originally in wood, were later imitated in stone. Round the dagoba were altars, called "Ayikas," at the four cardinal points, connected by an ambulatory, or processional way, encircling the shrine. Some of these are in existence to-day. Dagobas

The Lost Cities

were originally pierced by wooden pegs on which were entwined garlands of flowers, but now only the unrestored dagoba of great antiquity possesses holes in its surface, where the pegs once were, since, in later times, plaster garlands took the place of flowers, to the great loss in beauty of dagobas in general.

The traveller will also observe that dagobas assume different forms. The explanation is that, in the course of time, five different styles of dagobas were developed, imitating in their contours one of the following objects: a bell, an umbrella, a heap of paddy, a lotus-flower and a nello, which is a small round fruit. During the past centuries these shapes have become somewhat obscured, but the visitor may still find pleasure in speculating into which category an individual dagoba originally fell.

(b) *Tissamaharama*

Tissa is mentioned first of the "Lost Cities," being the most antique, but it is also the least important and, being rarely visited by the traveller owing to its comparative inaccessibility, little space can unfortunately be devoted to it here.

Originally known as "Magama," this was the earliest capital of Ceylon, and owes its foundation

Ceylon

to King Devanampiyatissa, "the darling of the gods." The city was built about 230 B.C., and to-day there are in existence four considerable monuments dating from that period. The most important is the Tissamaharama Dagoba which, being said to enshrine a relic of the Buddha, is still an object of pilgrimage. It is a great, bell-like structure built of brick and covered with pale blue plaster. The base of the *tee* is square and decorated with acanthus leaves, while large swags of fruit, curiously reminiscent of eighteenth-century Europe, ornament the upper part of the dagoba. The *ayikas*, although original in design, are much restored, and this magnificent dagoba is marred by hideous modern gates giving entrance to the enclosure. In its original glory, more than two thousand years ago, the Tissamaharama was hung with an immense frill of crochetwork as an adornment.

A smaller but exquisite erection is the "Manik" or "Pearl" Dagoba. Shaped like this jewel, it is covered with pale blue-grey plaster, and the *tee* is decorated with lotus leaves. This beautiful little dagoba also dates from the third century B.C., but it has frequently been replastered. Near by is the larger and more derelict "Jathale" Dagoba which has never been plastered, and the rose-coloured

The Lost Cities

bricks can be seen in their original condition. Across the face of this colourful dagoba are hung row upon row of little painted flags, which enliven, even if they tend to hide, the brick surface. On these flags are written messages for the Buddha. Although these are naturally supposed to be of a pious nature, they are sometimes said to express desires of a more mundane character.

The last object of interest at Tissamaharama is the Queen's Palace, where lived King Tissa's wife. Now only a mass of gaunt monoliths remain, reminiscent of the "Brazen Palace" at Anuradhapura, against a background of coconuts and jungle. It is a pity that more travellers do not visit Tissamaharama. It lies in beautiful surroundings some thirty miles from the entrance to the Yala game sanctuary.

(c) *Mihintale*

The Sacred Mountain, on which Mahinda converted King Tissa to Buddhism, is the gateway to Anuradhapura, both literally and historically, since it is situated eight miles east of that city on the main road to Trincomalee, and but for the fruitful meeting on its summit Anuradhapura would never have existed as a monument of Buddhist art. If the

Ceylon

traveller, as he probably will, approaches Mihintale from the city, he may reflect as he traverses this boiling and uninteresting road that nineteen hundred years ago it was carpeted the whole way, since that most solicitous of kings, Mahadathika-mahanaga, decided that, for the convenience of his subjects, Mihintale should be connected to Anuradhapura by carpets to prevent the soiling of their feet on pilgrimage.

The mountain lies a short distance to the right of the road, and on arrival at its foot a great golden flight of steps breaks the rocky surface. It is an arduous climb, but the traveller may be encouraged by the illusion that such a superb stairway must eventually lead to some celestial region. At the top of the first or lowest flight some less imposing steps lead on the right to the magnificent Kantaka Cetiya Dagoba which, since its restoration by the Archaeological Survey between 1934 and 1937, is by far the most important monument on Mihintale. Viewed from above it appears like a vast golden pudding, strangely reminiscent of schoolroom fare. It is finely situated on a plateau little bigger than itself, and surrounded by deep gullies and great rocks, where the unfriendly bear may be encountered at dawn and sunset.

5. The Kantaka Cetiya, Mihintale. View from the Naga Pokuna

6. "The Brazen Palace," Anuradhapura (See page 118)

The Lost Cities

The "Cetiya" was built in the reign of King Tissa (247 to 207 B.C.), and King Lanjatissa (59 to 50 B.C.) probably added the beautiful *ayikas* at the cardinal points. Each *ayikas* has two fringes of elephant's head or "Makaras" (fabulous and grotesque animals) exquisitely chiselled from white marble, which to-day is encrusted with bronze-coloured dust. I was fortunate enough to visit this dagoba at sunset and again at dawn (or perhaps a little later). In the morning it was shrouded from the sun by the mountain behind, and a great shadow darkened the expanse of jungle between the Sacred Mountain and Anaradhapura. At evening the sun illumined the plateau with a golden effulgence, detaching the "Cetiya" with its mellow light from the face of the dark mountain behind. The view across the dense jungle, split by silver tanks, to the distant jagged hills, behind which the crimson sun was slowly descending, was perhaps the finest I ever enjoyed in Ceylon.

It is pleasant to linger round the Kantaka Cetiya, particularly as the other objects of interest lie considerably higher up the mountain, but the traveller must now return to the top of the first flight of steps and ascend abruptly to a flat terrace, where several ruins can be seen. The columns of several Viharas and of a so-called "Alms-hall,"

Ceylon

perhaps a refectory for the *bhikkhus*, will be noticed, while a short distance further on by a terrace wall stands one of the finest pieces of sculpture in the island. This is the prancing lion holding up the stonework of a carved "Pokuna," or open-air bath. He is over seven feet in height and vigorously paws the air in the direction of his advancing admirer. The conception and craftsmanship of this figure are both superb. Unfortunately for the photographer, the lion prances in perpetual shade.

The exhausted traveller must now undertake another stiff climb in order to reach the umbrageous plateau on which lies the Ambasthala Dagoba. On arrival he will probably be grateful for the milk of a "Kurumba," or young coconut, fetched from an adjacent tree by an agile youth, before turning his attention to this dagoba with its glittering white exterior covering a brick core, which dates from the time of King Tissa (247 to 207 B.C.). The Ambasthala was later restored in the first century A.D. when, according to the Mahawamsa, there were set up at the entrances "four bejewelled arches, that had been well planned by artists and shone with gems of every kind." Across the face of the dagoba was draped "a cover of red stuff and golden balls and festoons of pearls."

The Lost Cities

Although naturally no trace of this splendour remains, the traveller will love this pretty little dagoba, which is surrounded by lolling monoliths and enshrines the relics of Mahinda. Above it towers the high black rock, now hung with the flags of the pious, where the "Thera" alighted after his arduous flight from India. It is called "Mahinda's bed," but it is improbable that even the austere "Thera" could have enjoyed much repose on its rocky surface.

On the western side of the plateau rises the rugged and decaying mass of the Mahasaya Dagoba, also dating from the third century B.C. and containing a hair from the "Urna," which is the name given to the space between the Buddha's eyebrows. From the summit of this dagoba the sturdy traveller can obtain a memorable view, but many may prefer to rest awhile on this shady and peaceful plateau before beginning the more important and exhausting climb to the Naga Pokuna, or Snake's bathing pool. The author, to his regret and shame, was too supine to attempt this expedition, but other writers, presumably less indolent, insist on the rare beauty of the great five-headed cobra carved in low relief on the rock above the water. He dates from the sixth century A.D., and his serpentine form is said to continue below the surface.

Ceylon

To see Mihintale thoroughly and in comfort two full days are necessary, and as there is no longer a rest-house there the traveller will probably stay at Anuradhapura. At the conclusion of his inspection of the dagobas on the "Sacred Mountain" he will doubtless praise their builders' foresight in placing them round the summit of a mountain, thereby combining penance with exercise both for the devout pilgrim and the inquiring visitor.

(d) Anuradhapura

This is the most important of the "Lost Cities," and is the first in the great trinity of beauty in the island, with Polonnaruwa and Sigiriya. In the section on the Mahawamsa the historical associations of Anuradhapura were briefly mentioned, and now each of the outstanding monuments will be described. As it is quite impossible for the novice to visit the "city" without a guide, little space has been allotted to topographical information.

The "Eight Sacred Places" come first in significance, and these include the more important ruins. They will therefore receive the principal attention, although for the sake of convenience ruins of lesser consequence, but in the same neighbourhood, will be grouped with them. These

The Lost Cities

eight places are sacred to Buddhists through their pre-eminent religious connections, and their preservation therefore rests, perhaps unfortunately, in the hands of the local *bhikkhus*, rather than in those of the authorities of the Archaeological Survey of Ceylon.

The first of the Sacred Places, in religious rather than in artistic importance, is the Bo-tree in the Mahavihara, or Great Temple, situated very near the centre of the modern town. The authenticated history of this august tree, which is well over two thousand years old, has been related in the previous chapter. It is therefore with a feeling of awe that one inspects its hoary beflagged surface, supported by iron posts and swaddled in coloured bandages, while an orange-clad *bhikkhu* anxiously watches one's shoeless and hatless progress round the uneven and sunbaked platform which surrounds it. This concerned attitude on the part of the priest is the result of various attacks made on the Bo-tree's sacred person. Indeed, only a few years ago a too zealous Singalese Catholic was discovered mutilating the tree with a hatchet; a profanation which was punished with imprisonment. The temple buildings which surround the Bo-tree are of comparatively little interest. At the bazaar end, however, of the Mahavihara rise the columns with

Ceylon

carved capitals of the so-called "Peacock Palace." This is not one of the sacred places, nor even a palace, but the ruins of a large Vihara, overshadowed by great banyans.

Directly to the left of the Bo-tree lie the ruins of the Lohapasada, or Brazen Palace, another sacred place. This was an immense monastery built by King Dutthagamani about 100 B.C. and, according to the Mahawamsa, it must have been one of the most remarkable buildings ever erected in any part of the world. The Lohapasada, which was nine storeys high, formed a square, each side being a hundred cubits long, while the height had a similar measurement. The whole of the exterior was covered with plates of copper, from which the Brazen Palace derived its name. The interior was divided into a thousand chambers, lighted by windows inlaid with coral lotus-flowers and hung with silver bells. In the middle of the building rose the Gem Pavilion shaped like a "God's chariot." It was supported by carved pillars of precious stone, and the walls were hung with a network of pearls. In this pavilion was erected an ivory throne with a seat of mountain-crystal, and in the back was fashioned the firmament of heaven: a sun in gold, a moon in silver, and stars of pearl. On the throne was placed a fan of ivory, and

The Lost Cities

above it a white parasol with a coral foot and a silver staff. The Mahawamsa concludes, not without reason: "Palace, parasol, throne and pavilion were beyond price." To-day one thousand six hundred stone monoliths, arranged in forty parallel lines, with forty columns in each, which formed the foundations of this astonishing edifice, are the only witnesses of its former glory. They stand up from the lush grass like a battalion of lank guardsmen, and their arrangement bears evidence to the tidy minds of the Archaeological Commissioners of Ceylon.

North-east of the Lohapasada rises the great Ruanweli, or "Gold-dust," Dagoba, as remarkable and as sacred as any building in the island. It was also erected by King Dutthagamani in order to enshrine the Sacred Footprint and to house a precious collection of the Buddha's relics. The most magnificent and largest dagoba in Ceylon, being two hundred and seventy feet high and two hundred and ninety-four feet in diameter, Ruanweli is built entirely of brick; but when it was restored in 1937 incorrect bricks were used, since it is unfortunately outside the supervision of the Archaeological Commissioners. It has the usual three storeys of ambulatories and an *ayika* at each cardinal point. In the distance it resembles a

Ceylon

colossal red balloon crowned with a dazzling white and golden *tee*, and on nearer approach the intermittent scaffolding straggling across its bulbous face seems to increase its magnitude and varifies its simple configuration.

Many pages of the Mahawamsa are filled with the details of the building of Ruanweli. At first King Dutthagamani was appalled at the prospect of securing sufficient bricks, but an obliging iguana led a huntsman to an unknown store of them in the jungle. The shape that the dagoba should assume also worried the monarch, but the resourceful master-builder produced, as if by magic, an immense bubble in a golden bowl. Dutthagamani was delighted and said, "Thus will I make it." Over a million *bhikkhus* attended the foundation ceremony, and "in the midst of the relic-chamber the King placed a Bodhi-tree made of jewels, splendid in every way. It had a stem eighteen cubits high and five branches; the root, made of coral, rested on sapphire. The stem of perfectly pure silver was adorned with leaves made of gems, had withered leaves and fruits of gold and young shoots made of coral." Over this resplendent tree a canopy was erected made of a "network of pearl bells and chains of little golden balls." By the Bodhi-tree Dutthagamani placed on a throne a

The Lost Cities

"shining golden Buddha-image seated. The body and members of this image were duly made of jewels of different colours, beautifully shining."

The enshrining of the relics was not an easy task, since a Naga, desiring to possess them himself, assumed the form of an unusually large snake (the Mahawamsa relates that its body was eight and a half miles in circumference) and, swallowing the urn containing the relics, the reptile retired into the jungle. Fortunately, however, his conscience soon pricked him, and disgorging the urn he returned it to the King. The relics could now be enshrined, and the chamber containing them was then closed by the *bhikkhus* with "fat-coloured stones." At the end of the ceremony the priests issued an edict saying that "the flowers here shall not wither, these perfumes shall not dry up; the lamps shall not be extinguished; nothing whatsoever shall perish; the six fat-coloured stones shall hold together for evermore." When the pious Dutthagamani came to die he commanded that he should be laid on a stone slab where, by turning first on his left and then on his right side, he could alternately see his two greatest and most beloved creations, the Ruanweli and the Lohapasada. Here he died, and to-day the slab near Ruanweli is pointed out to the visitor, who, if he

Ceylon

is not self-conscious, can perform the same action as the King.

On the east side of Ruanweli are seven statues, probably the finest in Ceylon, of which five line the gallery of a small Buddhist temple. The first on the left is a likeness of King Dutthagamani, while the remainder represent the four Buddhas who have visited the earth. The King, crowned with a pagoda-like hat and holding a lotus-flower, is a realistic and impressive figure. Of the four Buddhas, who in every case have the right hand raised, the second from Dutthagamani is outstanding. His left hand facing inwards is superbly worked, the folds of his garment are freely chiselled and painted in gold, while his slightly inclined head completes a work of the first sculptural importance. The fourth statue from the King should also be noticed, owing to the subtle indication of a belt beneath the robes. Before leaving the gallery the visitor should observe the contrast between the realistic representation of the King and the severely stylized forms of the Buddhas. A short distance from this temple stand two statues at the top of a short flight of steps. They represent King Dutthagamani and his mother. The outstanding feature of this beautiful representation of the King is the elegance of the folded hands which

The Lost Cities

incline perceptibly towards the chest. The body of his mother is arrayed in bangles and necklaces and crowned with a hat, apparently of Chinese origin. Her face is aloof and reposeful, and her profile is reminiscent of a primitive Italian Madonna. It would be impossible to exaggerate the beauty of these figures.

About two hundred yards north of Ruanweli lies the Thuparama Dagoba, one of the foremost of the "Eight Sacred Places." It is approached across a stretch of ground rather resembling the lay-out of a park in England, although timbered with very un-English trees. It was built by King Devanampiyatissa (247–207 B.C.) to enshrine the collar-bone of the Buddha. The core of this bell-shaped dagoba is the oldest in Ceylon, although the white plaster shell is comparatively modern. The dagoba, rising from a circular base, is forty feet in diameter and sixty-three feet high. The delicate beauty of the Thuparama is enhanced by the elegant monoliths, a hundred and thirty-four in number, which surround it. The original use of these columns is to-day a matter of speculation. They are too low to have supported a roof over the dagoba, but it is possible that they were hung with painted scenes from the Buddha's life, or else with garlands of flowers. At the foot of the steps

Ceylon

leading to the dagoba is a large cistern hewn out of a single block of stone. Here I once saw an orange-clad monk engaged in washing an extra robe against the dazzling white background of the dagoba. A hundred yards east of the Thuparama is another stone cistern which, according to tradition, was the drinking-trough of Dutthagamani's pugnacious but amiable elephant, Kandula.

Close to the Thuparama rise the fascinating ruins of the Dalada Maligawa, or Tooth Temple, which, despite the holiness of the relic it once housed, is not one of the sacred places. The story of the Buddha's venerated eye-tooth is told in the chapter on Buddhist shrines. These ruins, which, dating from the third century B.C. are probably the oldest at Anuradhapura, consist of the usual forest of gaunt columns on a slightly raised platform, and in the inner portion, where no doubt the tooth was preserved, they are crowned with open lantern-shaped heads which are said to represent teeth.

South-west of the Thuparama and behind the hotel rises the great brick structure of the Mirisawetiya Dagoba, another of the sacred places. It has been restored with funds given by that King of Siam who visited Ceylon in 1888. The main features of this rotund and rather prim-looking

The Lost Cities

dagoba are the beautiful high *ayikas* decorated in relief, of which the western is in the best state of repair. The name of this dagoba has a romantic origin. One day King Dutthagamani, while enjoying a picnic in the vicinity, omitted to share, as was his custom, his chillisambol with the crowd of monks which always accompanied this priest-loving King. As a penalty for this oversight he found, on returning from a bathe at Tissawewa, that his jewelled sceptre was so firmly fixed in the earth that human strength was unable to move it. Dutthagamani then remembered his discourtesy to the *bhikkhus* while at luncheon and, accepting this spiritual reprimand in a humble spirit, he commanded that a great dagoba should be erected over the sceptre. Thus was built the Mirisawetiya or "Chilli" Dagoba.

For the traveller whose powers of concentrated sight-seeing are limited there are two beautiful walks a short distance south of the Mirisawetiya, along the banks of the Tissawewa, that immense tank which also owes its origin to King Dutthagamani. One follows the high band to Isurumuniya (described in the chapter on Buddhist shrines) two miles distant, the other leads north past the tank and along the Outer Circular Road. The jungle here is very attractive, and the robust ruins

Ceylon

of some early "Viharas," or temples, in various stages of decay can be enjoyed on the way.

There are still three of the "Eight Sacred Places" to consider, of which two dagobas, the Abhayagiriya and the Jetawanarama, must be discussed in sequence despite their distance apart, since their names have been confused during the course of the centuries. The original Abhayagiriya, now called the Jetawanarama, and the most northerly of the dagobas, is a great unplastered mass of brickwork, shaped like a bell and two hundred and thirty feet high. It was originally built in 88 B.C., but it was enriched by King Maha Sena (A.D. 325–352), who crowned it with a jewelled *tee*. The nimble mind of Sir James Tennent, in his *Ceylon*, calculated that the bricks composing this dagoba would form a wall one foot in thickness and ten feet in height, reaching from London to Edinburgh. No doubt Sir James was right, but how he knew no one can say.

The Abhayagiriya, originally the Jetawanarama, which lies south-east of the Thuparama, was built by King Maha Sena and once was the largest dagoba in Anuradhapura, being four hundred and five feet high, which is fifty feet higher than St. Paul's Cathedral. To-day it is not more than two hundred and forty feet in height, and it is

The Lost Cities

the most dilapidated and picturesque dagoba in Anuradhapura. Flowering shrubs of many varieties clamber up its desiccated brick surface, while the *tee* is often smothered in lantana and jasmine. It is possible, but not easy, to climb to the summit of this unassuming dagoba. Almost midway between the Abhayagiriya and the Jetawanarama lies the Lankarama Dagoba, the last of the sacred places, which is said to have been built in A.D. 900. It is shaped like a teapot and encircled by three rows of beautiful columns similar to those round the Thuparama. This curious dagoba is surrounded by large trees, which are profusely inhabited by playful monkeys.

Having concluded this brief description of the "Eight Sacred Places" and of other monuments of less importance in their neighbourhood, I will now return with the visitor to the vicinity of the Jetawanarama, where many interesting remains can be seen. A short distance due west of this dagoba lie the ruins of a great "Vihara," incorrectly called the "King's Palace." What is left of these buildings, although well designed, is of little importance in comparison with the semi-circular "Moonstone" below the steps, which is the finest specimen in the island. The Ceylonese "Moonstone" is unique, and consists of a semi-circular slab of

Ceylon

carved stone worked in concentric rings. The example at the "King's Palace" contains an outermost ring of floral design. Next in a wider band is carved a procession of elephants, horses, lions, and bullocks following each other round the band in that order. It is interesting to observe that the elephants and bullocks, with which the artist must have been very familiar, are much more realistically carved than the horses, which were less common to him, and the lions, no specimen of which he could ever have seen. Inside the frieze of animals is another floral design, and within the latter a procession of "Hansa" or sacred geese. Each goose carries in its beak a trefoil lotus representing "Buddha, Dhamma and Samgha." They are busy and important-looking birds. The rest of the "Moonstone" is occupied by another band of floral design, and the conventional lotus-flower occupies the centre. This beautiful piece of carving is clearly the work of a great artist, and had it not been for the bare feet of the worshippers, it could never have retained its pristine elegance for over two thousand years.

Above the "Moonstone" rise the steps to the ruined floor of the temple, each tread being ornamented with gay little "ganas," or dwarfs, while on either side stand the entrance balustrades which

7. The "King's Palace," Anuradhapura

8. Moonstone, "King's Palace," Anuradhapura

The Lost Cities

are in the ubiquitous and strange "Makara" design. This resembles a scroll issuing from the mouth of a fabulous animal bearing some affinity to a crocodile. The "Makara," in Hindu mythology, is the vehicle of Varuna, the God of the Ocean, and it has always been a distinct feature of Asiatic art.

Close to the "King's Palace" lie the so-called "Elephant Stables," although it is certain that they were the abode of *bhikkhus* rather than of elephants. From a wide platform rise some high columns, similar to those at the Mirisawetiya Dagoba, at the summit of which are cut grooves twelve inches wide in which the beams supporting the roof rested. The chief interest of this ruin is the beautiful "Guardstone" which stands at the base. This name is derived from the laudable action of the cobra, which protected the head of the sleeping Buddha from the rays of the sun with its outspread hood. In consequence the defence of the Buddhist religion became the traditional right of the cobras, whose sovereign, called the Naga King, is usually the dominant figure on a "Guardstone." The example by the "Elephant Stables" is considered the finest in Ceylon. It is five feet high, with a semi-circular carved canopy enshrining the half-naked figure of the Naga king. Behind his head is carved the seven-hooded cobra, and the monarch

Ceylon

seems to be enjoying a dance. On the other side of the road the visitor will notice the large "Pokuna," or bathing pool, and now called because of its size the "Elephant Pokuna." Nearby are also two great "Stone Canoes," used by the monks for storing their food.

A short distance west of the "Elephant Stables" the so-called "Queen's Pavilion" should be seen. It is well situated on raised ground and contains some fine columns, although it is clearly the remains of a "Vihara" and was never connected with any queen. Before leaving this vicinity the visitor should inspect the "Kuttam Pokuna," or "Twin Baths," which lie north-east of the Jetawanarama. These beautiful baths, which look like large empty swimming pools, are both fifty-one feet wide, while the larger is a hundred and thirty-two and the smaller bath ninety-one feet long. The scroll balustrades leading down to them should be noticed by the visitor, who must reject as improbable the guide's inevitable assertion that the larger was called the "King's" and the smaller the "Queen's" bath. Once again it was the fortunate monks who possessed them. The exact date of the monuments just described is a little uncertain, but it must always be remembered that the greater part of Anuradhapura was built during

The Lost Cities

the reigns of Kings Dutthagamani and Tissa, which covered the years 101 to 44 B.C. It is therefore usually safe to assign any ruin to that period.

Having visited all the principal architectural and structural remains at Anuradhapura, we can now consider two sculptural objects of transcendent beauty in this great wilderness of ruins. I refer to the two famous sedent Buddhas; one between the "stone canoes" and the Jetawanarama, and the other about five hundred yards west of that dagoba. They are both isolated and unprotected in the jungle, except for the banyans around them, which offer some reverential shade. Again, these statues are both above life-size, are made of stone and seated on brick pedestals. Both figures and pedestals were restored 1936–7. The great hollow eyes denote the original presence of semi-precious stones, and certainly two thousand years ago these magnificent figures were as vulgarly painted as are all the figures of the Buddha to-day. They must also have been enshrined in ornate temples with lotus-flower canopies over their heads. But to-day, with a fortuitous but exquisite propriety, they represent more fully than ever in their past splendour the person of the Lord Buddha, whose birth, "Enlightenment," and missionary labours took place under the open sky.

Ceylon

These statues are of great artistic merit. The superb but unknown artists who chiselled them worked on an axis from the centre of the figure, being indifferent to the claims of realism, and content to indicate both the hair and garments of the Buddha with distinct but faint lines. The visitor will notice the pronounced length of the nose on both statues, which is an accepted indication of sanctity in the East, and he may be able to compare it in his mind with the impression of the same organ on the Holy Shroud at Turin. These figures symbolized for me the imperishable spirit of Anuradhapura, which even the depredations of the Tamils, the passing of the centuries, and the encroachment of the jungle have been unable to subdue.

As the traveller reluctantly prepares to leave Anuradhapura, he may like to recreate in his imagination the city as it was in the time of King Dutthagamani, two thousand years ago. At that time Anuradhapura covered an area of two hundred and fifty-six square miles, and the distance between the north and south gates of the city was sixteen miles. The population was approximately five and a half million, equal to the whole population of the island at the present time. In this great city which, according to a contemporary chroni-

The Lost Cities

cler, was "refulgent from the numerous temples and palaces, whose golden pinnacles glitter in the sky," the principal thoroughfares were called Moon Street, Great King Street, River Street, and Bullock Street. They were divided, as is customary in the East, into separate quarters for the various callings of drapers, goldsmiths, provision dealers and artisans. Of the streets the same chronicler wrote that their sides were "strewed with black sand, while the middle is sprinkled with white; they are spanned by arches of bending wood bearing flags of gold and silver, whilst vessels of the same metals containing flowers are observed on either side. In niches placed for the purpose are statues holding lamps."

According to the chronicler, these gorgeous streets formed the background of a lively scene, since "elephants, horses, carts and multitudes of people are ever to be seen, passing and repassing. There are dancers, jugglers and musicians of all kinds and of all nations; the latter performing on chank-shells ornamented with gold." While inside the city hospitals and almshouses were abundantly provided, outside lay great cemeteries and immense tracks of land consecrated to the growth of flowers with which to decorate the dagobas. It is pleasant to-day to gaze upon Ruanweli and to

Ceylon

imagine that vast dome covered perhaps with frangipani, hibiscus, jasmine, orchids, and lotus flowers, scenting the light breeze with an overwhelming and even nauseating perfume. With the exercise of a little fantasy the traveller may be able to recreate in his imagination some of the past splendours of the beautiful and opulent capital of Lanka.

(e) *Polonnaruwa*

Apart from the many centuries that separate their respective foundations and the diversity of their architectural styles, Polonnaruwa also profoundly differs from Anuradhapura since, while the ruins of the latter lie by a large town which is a centre of government, Polonnaruwa is situated in the heart of jungle from which it has only been partially rescued in recent years. To-day this once great capital of Ceylon is a "jungle city" in the most literal sense of the words, an incidence which adds great charm to the superb beauty of its ruined monuments. Indeed, only a short time ago it was considered prudent, before entering any building of which the interior could not be clearly seen, to herald one's approach by a shower of stones in order to drive away any bear which might be

The Lost Cities

awaiting, with malicious interest, the entrance of the unsuspecting visitor.

Although Polonnaruwa was originally built by the Cholas from southern India at the beginning of the eleventh century, only the ruins of one small Hindu temple bear witness to-day of that ephemeral rule. None of the other buildings in existence are earlier in date than the beginning of the twelfth century, after King Wijabahu I (A.D. 1070–1114) had conquered the city for the Singalese dynasty. It was, however, during the reign of his successor, the great Parakramabahu I (A.D. 1153–1186), that the great ecclesiastical buildings were erected, the ruins of which we are about to examine. While visiting these magnificent ruins the traveller may reflect with transitory interest on the strange coincidence that, at the same time Parakramabahu was building this city to glorify the religion of the Lord Buddha, the Cistercians in England were constructing abbeys and monasteries in the name of the Catholic Church. Both these great monuments of culture erected in the name of religion, although from diverse causes, are in a similar condition of ruin to-day.

For the convenience of the visitor I propose to begin the description of Polonnaruwa at its most

Ceylon

southernly point, and to work gradually to its northern extremity. Fortunately the ruins lie practically in a straight line running north and south, while the rest-house is found in the latter vicinity. A guide is, if possible, even more necessary here than at Anuradhapura, since large tracts of jungle sometimes separate the various buildings.

The Potgul Vehera, the most southernly ruin in Polonnaruwa, is thought to have contained the library of Rupavati, Parakrama's favourite queen, and has a circular room with the foundations of a fifteen-foot wall which, owing to its thickness, probably supported a dome. It was only sixty years ago that this building became a complete ruin, when thieves pillaged and destroyed it, searching for valuable books. Opposite the Vehera stands the stone statue of a bearded man eleven feet high, with a cap on his head and a sacred book in his hand. This beautiful work has already been mentioned as perhaps representing Parakramabahu himself. It is to be regretted that to-day the experts maintain that it is rather the figure of some obscure Hindu ascetic, and not the great king, holding in his hand a favourite volume from the adjacent library of his cultured queen. Thus are romantic notions dissipated by the advance of archaeological lore.

Some distance further north lie the ruins of the

9. Sedent Buddha, Anuradhapura (See page 131)

10. The Thuparama, Polonnaruwa (See page 138)

The Lost Cities

large brick palace of King Parakramabahu. It is one of the most imposing buildings in Polonnaruwa, and from the outside, owing to the curious formation of the crumbled brickwork, it resembles a line of "bustled" ladies in conference. The interior, which covers two hundred square feet, contains many large rooms and a well-preserved staircase, while the indications of water supply and sanitation are considerably in advance of those to be found in England at the same period. North-west of the palace is the Council Chamber, remarkable for the beautiful carvings of elephants, lions and dwarfs which adorn the exterior. This fascinating little building, which was excavated in 1905, appears to be built of sandstone, although it is actually of granite, mellowed by time into this soft yellow hue.

North-east of the Council Chamber are situated the ruins of the Siva Devale which, as has been mentioned, is the sole unearthed relic of the earlier Hindu domination. It is in the Dravidian or South Indian style of architecture, and it is thought that for a time this temple, which was originally dedicated to the worship of demons, actually enshrined the Sacred Tooth of the Lord Buddha. Indeed, to this day it is popularly called the Dalada Maligawa, or Temple of the Tooth.

Ceylon

A short distance north of the Siva Devale lies the great brick fabric of the Thuparama. Although this temple is influenced by Dravidian architecture, it was built as a Buddhist shrine and contains several mutilated statues of the Buddha. While the interior is plain the exterior walls are ornamented with small pilasters forming panels, in which are raised in plaster-relief shrine-niches and friezes of animals. The Thuparama, which has recently been restored with skill, is the only temple of any size at Polonnaruwa which still retains its roof intact. Opposite the Thuparama are situated the beautiful ruins of the Latamandapa, or "Flower-stem Hall," built during the reign of King Nissanka Malla (A.D. 1187–1196). It consists of a raised platform surrounded by a robust stone fence. In the centre rises a miniature dagoba, which is surrounded by a number of delicate columns with capitals resembling unopened flowers. No visitor should miss this exquisite little shrine.

To the east of the Latamandapa lies the Watadagé, or circular relic-house, one of the most beautiful and important monuments at Polonnaruwa. King Nissanka Malla was also responsible for this imposing building, which consists of two circular terraces one above the other. From the lower terrace four flights of stone steps at the

The Lost Cities

cardinal points lead to the upper one, on which are seated four images of the Buddha facing the four entrances. Each flight of steps possesses fine carvings of "Makaras," "Nagas," and dwarfs on the risers, although the latter, in their exaggerated attitudes, show a distinct aesthetic decline from their more restrained predecessors at Anuradhapura. The four Buddhas, each of whom was once protected by a wooden umbrella-shaped roof, are more remarkable for their romantic and derelict surroundings than for their artistic value. The Wata-dagé is mainly built of granite, weathered into a rich yellow hue, while the inner wall is of mellow red brick. In a brief, irresponsible moment this structure reminded me of a small open-air circus, with four seated clowns at the entrances to entertain their clients on arrival.

North of the Wata-dagé the visitor will observe one of the most curious buildings in Ceylon. This is the Sat-Mahal-Prasada, a six-storeyed building which originally had seven storeys, as its name implies. It tapers up into a small tower, and it is flanked by a stone staircase. Its purpose is uncertain, and the suggestion that it may have been used as a lighthouse seems untenable, considering it originally stood in the middle of a flourishing city more than thirty miles from the sea. Snakes

Ceylon

occasionally emerge from the obscure interior of this astonishing erection. Nearby lies the Hata-dagé, identified as the "Tooth Temple" of Polonnaruwa and built by King Nissanka Malla (A.D. 1187–1196). At the north end of a quantity of monoliths stands a mutilated figure of the Buddha. Just to the east of this temple is an enormous stone slab called the Gal-pota, or "Stone Book." It is twenty-six feet long, four feet wide, and it is estimated to weigh twenty-five tons. At each end a small stone relief shows Sri, the goddess of fortune, attended by two elephants. Shaped like an "ola" book, it records the virtues and achievements of Nissanka Malla, and also relates that this great stone was brought all the way from Mihintale, a distance of eighty miles. This king must have possessed some sturdy men.

A delightful walk can now be enjoyed northwards through the jungle in order to visit the remaining monuments at Polonnaruwa, although a primitive road is provided for the car of the indolent traveller. The first object of importance reached is the Rankot Vehera, which means the "Golden-spire Monastery." It is the largest and most magnificent dagoba at Polonnaruwa, being one hundred and eighty feet high and five hundred and fifty feet in circumference at the base. Built

11. The Lankatilaka, Polonnaruwa (See page 141)

12. Sedent Buddha, Gal-Vihara, Polonnaruwa (See page 142)

The Lost Cities

by Nissanka Malla at the close of the twelfth century, it is interesting to observe that it retains the archaic form of the earlier *stupas* of Anuradhapura. The Rankot Vehera is ornamented with *ayikas*, and the inscription states that this dagoba was originally surrounded by monks' quarters, walls and gateways, and was surmounted by a golden finial.

Some distance further north of this dagoba lies the Lankatilaka, or "Jewel of Ceylon" temple. Originally built by King Parakramabahu I (A.D. 1155–1186), and restored after a Tamil invasion by Wijabahu IV in 1275, this imposing brick temple, which, showing Dravidian influence, much resembles the Thuparama, is one hundred and seventy feet long and sixty-six feet wide. It is supposed to have been built on the model approved by the Buddha himself at Kapilavastu. The Lankatilaka is approached by two beautiful "Guardstones" and a broad flight of steps decorated with "ganas" on the risers. The massive walls of the interior still rise to a height of more than fifty feet, and in the sanctum stands a great brick and plaster figure of the Buddha without arms or head. This imposing ruin may remind the traveller of some roofless and desecrated English abbey. Opposite the entrance to the Lankatilaka lies a pretty little

Ceylon

temple called the Mandapaya Vihara, while further north rises the glistening form of the Kiri, or "Milk-white" Dagoba. It is the sister dagoba to the Rankot Vehera both in date and form. Originally it was coated with plaster and glistened like white marble.

North-west of this dagoba lie the superb rock-hewn figures of the Buddha and his favourite disciple Ananda, known as the Gal, or "Black rock," Vehera, which is perhaps the most impressive sight at Polonnaruwa. It dates from the reign of Parakramabahu I. On emerging into a clearing in the jungle the visitor will be amazed to see three immense black statues placed, as if at random, against the rock background from which they are hewn. On the left is a great sedent Buddha by a small rock temple. Further to the right there are two co-related figures of unique interest. The first, which is twenty-two feet high, is that of Ananda, who stands, a picture of resigned grief, with his eyes averted from the recumbent form of his dying master. This statue of the "Nirvana" is the largest in Ceylon, being forty-four feet long. The Buddha lies, as always, on his right side, with his head, supported on his right hand, lying on a pillow. The left arm is extended along his body, and lotus flowers ornament the soles of his feet.

The Lost Cities

The great size of the statue seems to emphasize the large feminine hips and the position of discomfort noticeable in every "Nirvana," while his Kaffir-like hair stands out with startling realism. It is awe-inspiring to realize that these great statues, now isolated in the depths of the jungle, were once highly painted, set with jewelled eyes and enshrined in a gorgeous temple in the centre of the capital of Lanka.

For the energetic traveller two further objects of interest can be visited before leaving Polonnaruwa. These are the lotus-bath and the temple called Demala-Maha-Seya. The former lies four miles from the rest-house, north of the Gal Vehera, and the latter is in the same vicinity. The lotus-bath, which dates from the twelfth century, must surely be one of the prettiest ponds in existence. It measures twenty-four feet nine inches across the top and drops to a depth of four feet six inches in five contracting circles, each carved to resemble the petals of the lotus flower, to form a small bath at the base with a diameter of five feet and four inches. In the report of the Archaeological Survey of Ceylon for 1909 the beauty of the lotus-bath is thus described: "Imagine a gigantic lotus flower of granite," wrote Mr. Bell, the Commissioner of that period, "full-blown . . . with

Ceylon

five concentric lamina of eight petals, gradually diminishing to a stamen. Then decide to reverse nature's order, and instead of a convex shape, depress the petal rings into a concavity. . . . We have the granite bath as it exists in all this shapeliness to this day."

Further north lies the last building of importance at Polonnaruwa: the Demala-Maha-Seya, built by the Cholas of southern India in the eleventh century. This brick temple shows the same Dravidian influence as the Thuparama and the Lankatilaka, and also contains a mutilated figure of the Buddha in the sanctum. It is, however, for the frescoes, sadly impaired by centuries of neglect, that this temple is famous. They represent scenes from the "Jatakas," which form the legends of the Buddha's previous incarnations. The best known is that of the hare (a humble disguise once assumed by the Master), who offered her own body to satisfy the appetite of a hungry man. The visitor will notice that orange and red with a pale blue-green were the artists' favourite colours, while the men are painted as belonging to a Nordic rather than to an Asiatic race.

On concluding his visits to the superb ruins at Polonnaruwa the visitor should recollect that, shortly after the death of King Nissanka Malla in

The Lost Cities

1196, the Tamils finally destroyed the city. It was only during the present century that excavations were undertaken by the authorities of the Archaeological Survey, who have been greatly assisted in their activities by the fortunate incidence that, unlike the dagobas at Anuradhapura, all the ruins at Polonnaruwa are under Government control, and not subject to the less knowledgable and more dilatory management of the Buddhist priests.

(f) Yapahuwa

After the eclipse of Polonnaruwa, Yapahuwa enjoyed an ephemeral glory by becoming the capital of Lanka. It was King Bhuvanekabahu I (A.D. 1277–1284) who decided to build a city on the slope of this natural rock fortress, and he was responsible for the erection of the Tooth Temple and the Royal Palace, of which the latter's magnificent stairway alone remains to-day. There are three flights to this royal approach, which climb up the luxuriant face of the mountain, and the highest of these is not only unique but as richly carved as any monument in Ceylon. There are thirty-five narrow steps, with deep risers and a wide balustrade on either side, initiated by two

Ceylon

delightful female figures, each holding a bowl of flowers in her hands. Half-way up are seated the "animal warders" of the stairway, represented by two stylized lions leering downwards at the approaching visitor. At the summit are several fluted columns which supported the entrance roof and an elegant porch with a doorway and windows on either side. The spirited frieze of dancing figures and the elaborately embellished pediments enhance the beauty of the design. The sides of this great construction are freely carved, and their supports have pagoda-shaped bases.

On passing through the stately entrance the visitor will find to his amazement that the royal stairway leads to nothing, except a small green plateau backed by a towering black mountain. The abrupt and unexpected end to such a magnificent approach increases the romantic and scenic fascination of this remarkable erection.

The life of Yapahuwa as the capital of Lanka only lasted to the death of King Bhuvanekabahu in 1284, when it was subjugated and despoiled by another Tamil invasion. It is, however, to the Portuguese that the odium of the final destruction of Yapahuwa pertains, since they plundered it ruthlessly in their search for treasure in the six-

The Lost Cities

teenth century. After Yapahuwa, Cotta, and then Kandy became in turn the capitals of Lanka; but to Yapahuwa belongs the distinction of being the most recent, as Tissamaharama is the most ancient, of the "Lost Cities" of Ceylon.

Chapter Six

SIGIRIYA, OR THE LION ROCK

☼

A visit to Ceylon would not be wasted if, amongst all its ornaments of antiquity, Sigiriya alone was visited. Ruined buildings of different ages are ubiquitous, but it is doubtful if anywhere a parallel could be found to this great rock palace, with its unique historical and artistic associations. Before describing the individual beauties of Sigiriya it will be appropriate briefly to relate the stirring events to which the palace owes its existence.

King Dhatu Sena, who succeeded in freeing his country of the Tamils in about the year A.D. 460, possessed two sons and one daughter. Of the former, Kasyapa was the child of a woman of inferior birth, while his younger brother Mogallana was born of a royal mother. The King's daughter was married to his commander-in-chief, Migara, but the latter was a very irascible soldier, and one day exceeded his conjugal rights, in the eyes of his father-in-law, by beating his wife "on her thighs with a whip" until she bled. The King,

13. The Recumbent Buddha, Gal-Vihara, Polonnaruwa (See page 142)

14. The Royal Stairway, Yapahuwa (See page 145)

Sigiriya, or the Lion Rock

hearing of this, ordered Migara's mother to be burnt alive. Incensed by his mother's death, Migara then revolted against Dhatu Sena and, together with Kasyapa who supported the commander-in-chief, they obtained possession of the King's person and, having stripped him naked and bound him with chains, Kasyapa with his own hands buried his father alive.

These hasty actions naturally caused a rift in the Singalese Royal Family, although Kasyapa's patricide possessed an element of poetic justice since Dhatu Sena, always an impatient man, had once ordered a seated *bhikkhu* to be buried alive, being desirous of building a tank on the exact place where the priest was absorbed in his meditations. After his father's death Mogallana, afraid of sharing a similar fate, escaped to India, while Kasyapa, although now King of Lanka, was driven by his guilty conscience to find a safer residence than Anuradhapura, in order to gain security from any future attempt of vengeance on his brother's part. Kasyapa therefore decided to resort to an inaccessible rock in the Matale district, on the summit of which he built a great brick palace named "Sihagiri," now contracted into Sigiriya, meaning the "Lion Rock." The palace was given this name on account of the stairway structure

Ceylon

ascending it, which was built in the form of a colossal lion. It is now time to consider the palace itself.

The visitor will be well advised to arrive at the rest-house at Sigiriya at sunset. He will then, if he is fortunate, see a great rock rising abruptly out of the forest-clad plain which, under the light of the setting sun, will appear like some fabulous black mushroom streaked with gold. The traveller will rise at dawn, since the ascent of Sigiriya—it is six hundred feet to the summit—is practically impossible under the midday sun, and a mile's walk will bring him to the foot of the mountain. On the way he may like to visit the Sigiriya Dagoba, which lies a short distance from the rest-house and a hundred yards from the road. This modest dagoba, excavated in 1910, contains a very interesting "Maha-meru-gala," or round stone pedestal, one foot three inches in height, which is profusely carved with scenes of village life. The size of the bricks used in this dagoba would indicate the ninth or tenth century as the period of its construction.

The path at the foot of Sigiriya first passes on the left the Cobra Rock, King Kasyapa's ceremonial bath and a low throne, standing on the stone foundations of the supposed Audience Hall. I have

Sigiriya, or the Lion Rock

been told that this seat is similar to the Lion Throne at Mahabalipuram in southern India. Shortly after the visitor will enter the passage on the western side of the rock, known as the lower gallery. This was the only way of approaching the palace on the summit, and its construction by Kasyapa's workmen was a masterpiece of engineering skill. Of the original gallery only a hundred yards remain. It is four feet six inches wide, sheltered by a high parapet wall of plastered brick. The plaster is so highly polished that even after one thousand five hundred years it retains its powers of reflection.

From this lower gallery the intrepid visitor can ascend fifty feet up a vertical iron ladder to a natural "pocket" in the rock, where he can enjoy some of the most beautiful frescoes to be seen in the East, and the only early Singalese paintings of outstanding merit in such an excellent state of preservation. These frescoes, which consist of twenty-one female figures of three-quarter length, were probably painted by monks early in the sixth century A.D. shortly after the death of Kasyapa, and they are executed in a similar style to the famous paintings at Ajanta in Hyderabad, which were executed about a hundred years later. Earlier authorities have suggested that these fascinating

Ceylon

ladies were celestial bodies owing to the clouds which gather round their knees, but it is now realized that the clouds were an artistic device to finish the figures owing to the lack of space on the rock's surface, which prevented the inclusion of their lower limbs. Authoritative opinion of the present day is that the frescoes are portraits of the ladies of Kasyapa's court, attended by their maids who are carrying baskets of flowers, on their way to the Vehera at Piduragala, which lies on a conical hill north of Sigiriya. If that is so, they must have formed a most graceful and voluptuous body of pilgrims.

Clearly these frescoes are the work of a great artist with a profound knowledge of colour and craftsmanship, since the line work in particular, which was executed with a brush, exhibits a high degree of artistic ability. Although from a cursory glance it might appear that these full-breasted women are naked from the waist upwards except for jewellery, a closer inspection will reveal that every torso is covered with a garment of filmy gauze. Their skins vary in colour as much as their features in outline; two elements which clearly indicate the cosmopolitan character of Kasyapa's court. The yellow and orange hues of the ladies' skins coincide with Aryan and Mongolian features,

15. *Sigiriya (See page 150)*

16. Frescoes, Sigiriya (See page 151)

Sigiriya, or the Lion Rock

while the blue-green tints used for the serving-maids assign them to a darker-skinned race. The discovery of these superb frescoes painted on the wall of an open cave, and high up the surface of this ostensibly inaccessible mountain, should provide the traveller with as keen an enjoyment as any other objects of beauty in Ceylon. There are also traces of other frescoes at Sigiriya, and it is said that in the time of Kasyapa there was a picture three hundred feet long and one hundred feet wide painted across the bleak western front of the mountain.

Returning from the cave of the frescoes to the lower gallery the climb is continued until the northern plateau is reached. This plateau is dominated by the two paws of the lion which alone remain of the great staircase structure, which in the form of a lion once reared its colossal height up the side of the mountain. In the lion's chest was the entrance door to the palace and other buildings on the summit of Sigiriya. The mammoth size of this unique concept of King Kasyapa can be judged by the two brick paws, which are over four feet high. But even with these indications of magnitude it is difficult to visualize Kasyapa's lion in his original grandeur gazing in defiance across the plain at the enemies, and receiving into safety

Ceylon

through his spacious chest the friends and followers of the King.

To the left of the paws rises a black cliff, to which are invariably clinging several of the largest and most formidable swarms of wild bees, "bambaras" in species, which the visitor may ever have seen. They reminded me of fabulous velvet reticules heaving on the black skirt of a Victorian giantess. These intimidating swarms should at once indicate to the traveller the practical value of the wire cage on the plateau, which in the case of emergency can hold six people. The bees are unlikely to prove hostile unless disturbed by monkeys or small boys, but many years ago they attacked a party of visitors which included the Duke and Duchess of Connaught. History relates that the Governor's daughter was standing on the rock high above the northern plateau, when on looking down she saw to her astonishment her father pursuing the Duchess of Connaught and vigorously beating her with his hat. At that distance the bees which were attacking the Duchess were invisible to the Governor's daughter, who therefore received the painful impression that her distinguished father had taken leave of his senses.

With this story in mind the traveller may ascend the rock above the northern plateau, on a path

Sigiriya, or the Lion Rock

which incidentally passes over the bees, with some trepidation, particularly when, having left the friendly rungs of an iron ladder, he is compelled to scale the mountain with only the aid of a single rail and a series of footholes cut horizontally in the rock. Escape from the bees would clearly be impossible in such circumstances but, provided they remain quiescent, the ascent for those not prone to vertigo is of an arduous rather than of an alarming character.

Once on the summit of Sigiriya the traveller will feel he is on the top of the world. It is so baked by the sun and swept by the wind that he may find it hard to realize that once this plateau was the site of a small city which housed King Kasyapa and his court. To-day only the foundations of these numerous buildings remain, but the pink granite throne of the King, discovered in 1895, still ornaments the ruins of his water-garden. This throne lies on the eastern side of the mountain, and the traveller may be tempted to visualize Kasyapa on its rosy but unyielding surface dispensing justice to the inhabitants of his rock kingdom, or else with the guilty reflections of a patricide in his heart awaiting with misgivings the dawn.

The whole of this romantic plateau was once

Ceylon

covered with brick buildings comprising the royal palace, courtyards and houses for the King's ladies and other members of the household. It was enclosed by a solid brick wall round the edge of the plateau. There was a plentiful supply of rain-water, which was collected by several artificial tanks constructed in natural depressions of the rock. The largest of these lies to the south of the throne on raised ground. As the various tanks were on different levels, numerous flights of stone steps radiating from this central point led to all the buildings served with water. When it is remembered that most of these steps and all the slats of white limestone, together with every brick, tile and piece of timber, used for the construction of these edifices on the summit of Sigiriya were brought from the plain and up the lower gallery just traversed by the visitor, the magnitude of King Kasyapa's achievement can be more fully appraised.

Before passing to the defeat and death of this king and the subsequent abandonment of Sigiriya, it may be interesting to note that during the excavations on the summit of the mountain, carried on since the end of the nineteenth century, over one thousand six hundred coins have been discovered. Of these all but twelve were of Roman

17. The Lion's Claw, Sigiriya (See page 153)

18. Temple of the Tooth, Kandy (See page 164)

Sigiriya, or the Lion Rock

origin, and they dated from the years A.D. 317 to 423. It is fascinating to realize that over one thousand five hundred years ago the same coinage must have been current in England, then under Roman rule, and in Kasyapa's Lanka.

Such was the unique and beautiful fortress-palace in which King Kasyapa ruled for eighteen years, approximately from A.D. 460 to 478 and, according to the chronicle, "in fear of the world to come and of Mogallana." And one day in the latter year these fears were realized. Perhaps it was dawn, and the King was sitting in his garden on his pink granite throne, when the faint light of the rising sun illumined for him a distant forest of moving spears crossing the jungle north of Sigiriya. Then as the sun rose higher King Kasyapa knew that it was his brother Mogallana, returned from India, advancing with a great army to give battle to his father's murderer. Either through vanity nurtured by flattery or through panic engendered by guilt, Kasyapa left his impregnable fortress and went down to the plain with his army to fight; perhaps with an added fear and bitterness in the knowledge that, while he, Kasyapa, was the son of a low-born woman, Mogallana was the offspring of a queen.

Each brother was mounted on an elephant for

Ceylon

the conflict, and perhaps each prayed that his own beast would emulate the prowess of Dutthagamani's Kandula. The chronicle says that the rival "armies met like two seas that had burst their bound," and for a while the fortunes of battle were equally shared by both. Defeat then overwhelmed Kasyapa inadvertently. His elephant, while negotiating a swamp, was compelled to turn his back on the enemy troops who, greatly encouraged by an action which they interpreted as retreat, hurled themselves with renewed vigour on the King's men and utterly defeated them. Kasyapa, in order to avoid the ignominy of capture, expedited his inevitable fate by cutting his throat with his own sword. Nevertheless, despite the defeat and death of Kasyapa, Mogallana was so enraged by the sight of those who had supported his father's murderer, that he gnashed his teeth at them with such violence that one of his front teeth permanently protruded from his mouth from that day. Not without cause, therefore, did Mogallana acquire the nickname of "Rakkhasa," which means a demon.

After his victory Mogallana was crowned King of Lanka at Sigiriya, but being unafflicted with the guilty conscience of Kasyapa he had no cause to isolate himself on the summit of the Lion Rock.

Sigiriya, or the Lion Rock

He therefore went to live at Anuradhapura, like his royal ancestors, and handed over Sigiriya to a confraternity of *bhikkhus*. It was then that these monks, as if wishing to recapture the hedonistic spirit of their predecessors, painted those exquisite frescoes on the rock. Perchance it was modesty that compelled them to choose such an inaccessible place for their artistic labours, particularly as the subjects they selected were of a mundane rather than of a pious nature. But perhaps they felt that, provided the ladies were depicted on a pilgrimage, they were justified in furnishing them with all the carnal virtues that their appetites could desire.

The *bhikkhus* were not long at the Lion Rock. It was too large and inconvenient for a religious confraternity. So for nearly one thousand five hundred years deserted Sigiriya suffered the cruel depredations of wind and rain and the inexorable encroachment of the jungle. It was only at the end of the nineteenth century that the excavation work was undertaken which to-day enables the visitor to enjoy in comfort and safety the unique beauty of the Lion Rock.

Chapter Seven

SOME BUDDHIST TEMPLES

☼

(a) *The Dalada Maligawa, or Temple of the Tooth, and the Nata Dewala, the Maha Dewala, the Malwatta and the Degaldoruwa temples at Kandy.*

A temple is fundamentally at variance with the Buddhist religion, since they were built to house statues of the Buddha which he himself had expressly forbidden to be made. In the first section of the chapter on the "Lost Cities" it was pointed out that the *stupa*, which later developed into the dagoba, enshrining relics of the Buddha, was the original object of worship amongst Buddhists. In the second century A.D., however, Buddha images were introduced which needed temples to enshrine them and, in the course of time as Buddhism became more idolatrous, these temples took the place of dagobas as popular places of worship. In India nemesis overtook this prostitution of the pure Buddhist faith, since by A.D. 700 the country which had given birth to the Buddha and first

Some Buddhist Temples

accepted his tenets had relapsed into the polytheistic Hinduism from which Buddhism had originally sprung. Hinduism had fatally corrupted and thereby destroyed Buddhism, but in return it had absorbed in the process sufficient knowledge of the ethical teaching of that religion as to recognize the Buddha as one of the ten incarnations of Vishnu. Buddhism in Ceylon, however, escaped similar extinction, and there are many temples in the island to-day which bear witness to its virility, impaired as it is by polytheistic accretions. Of these the most famous is the Temple of the Tooth at Kandy, but before describing it in detail the history of the Sacred Tooth which it enshrines will be briefly related.

The eye-tooth of the Lord Buddha was brought to Ceylon in A.D. 311 in the hair of a Brahmin princess and lodged in the Dalada Maligawa at Anuradhapura. Although the Bo-tree and the collar-bone had previously been the most venerated of the relics, it would appear that the Sacred Tooth at once usurped their position, and from that time until the present day it has been the central pivot of the Buddhist faith in Ceylon. Indeed, through the ages its possession by the King of Lanka was an essential asset to his authority, and when the *bhikkhus* who guarded it wished at any time to

Ceylon

bring pressure to bear on the monarch they had only to abscond with the Sacred Tooth to secure instant compliance with their desires.

When Anuradhapura was evacuated the Tooth was taken to Polonnaruwa, where in the twelfth century an aunt of the great Parakramabahu had the effrontery to steal it and to attempt to escape with the precious relic to India. How the King recovered it and how he punished his impious aunt are unfortunately unknown; but in the fourteenth century, after a sojourn at Yapahuwa, it was in fact stolen, presumably from Kotta, then the capital of Lanka, and taken to India. In order to recover it King Parakrama Bahu III actually was compelled to go to India in person, where he successfully pleaded for its return. A supreme disaster, however, befell the Sacred Tooth at Kotta in 1560, when it was seized by the Portuguese, borne in triumph to Goa, where it was burnt by the Archbishop himself in the presence of the Viceroy of the King of Portugal.

Thus was destroyed the probably genuine eye-tooth of the Lord Buddha, the most precious possession in the kingdom of Lanka. But neither the king of the day, Wikramabahu, nor the *bhikkhus* proposed to admit the truth of this sacrilege, and a few years after its destruction the

Some Buddhist Temples

Sacred Tooth mysteriously reappeared in Kandy, where in 1566 it was housed in the present inner shrine of the Dalada Maligawa, or Tooth Temple.

The new relic received then as it receives to-day the fervid worship of the credulous Buddhists, although it has no claims whatever to authenticity. The actual relic itself can only be closely inspected by the most exalted Buddhists, or in the distance by the multitude in the uncertain light of a Perahera, the annual August festival held in its honour. In the Colombo Museum, however, there is an exact replica of the Tooth springing from the heart of a lotus flower. It is nearly three inches in height and the thickness of a man's little finger. Clearly this relic could never have belonged to the mouth of any human being and, if a tooth at all, it must have originated in the jaw of some pre-historic animal. Little credit can be given to King Wikramabahu and his *bhikkhus* who, in the sixteenth century, showed so little good taste or imagination that they did not even take the trouble to secure a human tooth to take the place of that of the Buddha. Perhaps, however, they had a sense of humour.

The present Dalada Maligawa at Kandy dates from different periods. The inner shrine, which has housed the Tooth since the reign of Wikrama-

Ceylon

bahu, was probably erected in the fourteenth century, but the outer temples are of later construction. King Wimala Dhamma Suriya II (1687–1707) built a three-storeyed temple round the inner shrine, but apparently with unsatisfactory materials, since, owing to its rapid decay, his son King Narenda Sinha (1707–1739) was compelled to rebuild it in the two storeys which exist to-day. The only later addition was the delightful octagonal library on the right wing, which was erected early in the nineteenth century by Sri Wikrema Raja Sinha, the last King of Kandy.

The exterior of the Tooth Temple is a picturesque rather than an imposing construction, and the grey moated walls on the approach side are slightly reminiscent of a medieval French château. Tortoises loll in the sun where the sloping walls disappear into the moat, and a crowd of guides and beggars do likewise on the flight of steps which leads into the interior. The visitor first passes through an open lobby, where the tortures of Buddhists in hell between metapsychoses are painted in a realistic but primitive manner. The most savage punishment seems to be inflicted on those guilty of having taken animal life. Depicted in naked human form, golden skewers are being run through their puce-coloured bodies by bright

Some Buddhist Temples

blue devils. Passing into the inner courtyard the visitor will find himself in the main body of the building, in the centre of which stands the shrine of the Tooth. Around the walls recumbent, sedent and preaching Buddhas abound, painted in the crudest colours. The altars will be covered with blooms from the scarlet "Flamboyant" and the white "Frangipani," while the air will be heavy with the luscious smell of the "Temple Flower." In a shrine on the left there is a beautiful crystal Buddha with which, if he looks prosperous, the visitor will undoubtedly become acquainted.

Before inspecting the shrine of the Tooth it is usual to be taken upstairs to inspect the octagon library, which contains a fine collection of Oriental books. Here the traveller will be met by a suave and senior *bhikkhu*, who will show him some beautiful specimens of "olas," as these books are called. They are formed of dried strips of talipot leaves and bound in gem-studded silver covers. The *bhikkhu* will then demonstrate the method of writing in these books by inscribing with a style on a small leaf the visitor's name, which will become visible when a preparation of charcoal ground with oil is applied to it. Amongst other garish treasures a gilded leaf from the original Bo-tree at Gautama, and presented to the temple

Ceylon

by Edwin Arnold, will be shown by the *bhikkhu*, who will then open the visitors' book and proudly point out some distinguished names, which I remember include those of King Edward VII and Messrs. Lloyd George and Bernard Shaw. As the traveller is about to leave the *bhikkhu* will open a drawer displaying a five-rupee note. Any doubts, therefore, which he may have entertained as to the propriety of tipping such a grave and important individual will thereby be dispelled.

Returning to the main body of the building the visitor will now inspect the shrine containing the Sacred Tooth. This small rectangular edifice has an elaborately carved and crudely coloured roof, but the entrance doors, painted in a delicate pink and ornamented with golden peacocks, are very attractive. The granite surrounds to these doors are finely carved and probably date from the fourteenth century. Inside this rather pretentious building lies of course the Sacred Tooth of the Buddha. It is enshrined in seven "Karanduas," or caskets, inlaid with precious stones, each fitting into the other with the same diminishing and fascinating accuracy as those egg-shaped German toys which delighted so many an Edwardian childhood. In the smallest and innermost casket reposes the Sacred Tooth, springing from the heart of a golden lotus.

Some Buddhist Temples

It is only on three occasions in the year that the Tooth is exhibited to the public: on Wesak in May (the birthday, "Enlightenment," and death of the Buddha), on Poson in June (the arrival of Mahinda in Ceylon), and on the Perahera in August. Although the origin of the last-mentioned festival is unknown to-day, it is by far the most important of the three since, besides the exhibition of the Tooth, celebrations lasting ten days take place in Kandy which excite great religious fervour amongst the Buddhists of Ceylon. The main feature of the festival is the nightly procession through the town led by a particularly large and sagacious elephant, his tusks sheathed in gilt cases, bearing a golden palanquin on which rests the shrine containing the Sacred Tooth. Each night the enthusiasm of the people increases, and on the last before the full moon, as many as a hundred richly caparisoned elephants may take part in the procession. I hope the traveller will enjoy better fortune than myself, and be able to attend the August Perahera at Kandy.

On leaving the Dalada Maligawa the visitor should cross the road to the Nata Dewala opposite. A "Dewala," signifying a temple dedicated to various Hindu deities, shows the pollution which Buddhism has suffered from polytheistic sources.

Ceylon

The grounds of this temple are ornamented with a small dagoba, said to contain the alms bowl of the Buddha once housed in the Ruanweli at Anuradhapura, and several small shrines containing particularly garish Buddha images. One in particular may prove a severe test of the visitor's gravity. A large recumbent Buddha, painted yellow and magenta, gazes with startled eyes on the mourning figures of his disciples, who in various postures of grief are mopping their eyes with real lace handkerchiefs. The exact date of the Nata Dewala is unknown, but it appears to be earlier than the main building of the Dalada Maligawa, and probably dates from the early seventeenth century.

Three other temples should be visited by the traveller before leaving Kandy. The Maha Dewala, which lies to the right of the King's Pavilion, contains some fine jewels and a flag embroidered with the arms of the Dutch East India Company. The Malwatta temple is situated on the opposite side of the lake to the Dalada Maligawa. It contains a spacious "Poya-gé," or preaching hall, and if the visitor is in Kandy in June he should try to be present at a consecration of *bhikkhus* in this hall. It is a very colourful spectacle. The last temple of note in Kandy is the Degaldoruwa, just outside the town. The Lewella ferry must be crossed,

Some Buddhist Temples

followed by a walk of a mile and a half. This is a rock temple with an imposing recumbent Buddha and some fine wall paintings probably dating from the sixteenth century. With the exception of the Dalada Maligawa these temples are of comparatively little historical or architectural importance, but by visiting them the traveller will obtain some knowledge of the practice of Buddhism at the present day.

(b) Dambulla

This is the most remarkable rock temple in Ceylon. It consists in fact of five separate temples, dating from the reign of King Walagambahu in the first century B.C. They are approached over a great slope of black rock a short distance from the village of Dambulla, and on passing under a brick gateway the traveller will find himself on a high rock platform with the temple buildings on his right, and on the left a magnificent view over the jungle, with distant Sigiriya looking like a small mushroom in a north-easterly direction. This terrace is a favourite haunt of monkeys who, if the traveller is unfortunate, may playfully disappear with one of his shoes while he is making his pious and bare-footed progress round the temples.

Ceylon

The first temple shown contains the famous recumbent figure of the Buddha, cut out of the rock and contemporary with the foundation of the monastery. This image is forty-two feet long, and seen by the light of a solitary candle he presents, with his wide black eyes, a grim and savage appearance. Unlike most of the statues at Dambulla which were cruelly repainted about 1915, this Buddha retains most of the original faded paint. From the point of view of proportion, the visitor will be amazed at the size of this figure cut in a temple which should hardly contain an image of half that magnitude. This temple is called the Dewa Raja Vehera, which means the temple of the Great God, Vishnu, and indeed by the head of the recumbent Buddha there stands a great statue of this god. It is considered to be of equal sanctity with the Buddha image, and the presence of Vishnu in this temple comes as a considerable shock to anyone unaware of the corruption of the Buddhist religion.

The next temple, which is a natural cave and larger than the first, also contains a Buddha carved from the rock and fifty-eight painted statues mostly of clay. There are also some most interesting frescoes on the walls and ceiling representing various scenes from Singalese history. The visitor

Some Buddhist Temples

will probably be most attracted by those depicting the victory of King Dutthagamani over the Tamil Elara. Some of these frescoes date from the foundation of the temple, and are said to have been carried out by monks from Anuradhapura. The student familiar with Asiatic art will notice the strong Grecian influence in some of the figures, derived through the early Gandhara period of Indian art (50 B.C. to A.D. 500). These frescoes make this temple the most interesting, and the great array of crudely painted statues the most uncanny of all the temples at Dambulla.

The third temple is called the Maha Alut Vehera, or the Great New temple, and amongst a great wealth of statuary it contains two notable wooden figures of the founder, King Walagambahu, and his queen. The last two temples are of more modest proportions. One contains the effigy of an eighteenth-century Kandyan monarch, and the other a recumbent Buddha of the same period. This figure is made of brick and plaster, and European influence can be observed in the style of painting, particularly of the massive pillow supporting the head, which is decorated with little flowers. It is an unimportant but unusual image.

The visitor to Dambulla is strongly advised to provide himself with a quantity of small change,

Ceylon

since in every temple he will be expected to place a coin in the plate of an expectant *bhikkhu*. This is a maddening arrangement which, together with the heat and the discomfort of a shoeless progress, is liable to be a severe test of a European patience.

(c) *Isurumuniya*

This strange and irregular medley of buildings, at the foot and on the face of a high black rock, is situated in the outskirts of Anuradhapura, on the east side of the Tissawewa embankment. Although probably dating back to the reign of King Tissa (247–207 B.C.), it has been much restored throughout the centuries. As the traveller approaches Isurumuniya he will see on the left a large modern preaching hall, in the centre a high cliff on which is perched a small temple half-way up its surface, and on the right a tank measuring seventy-six square feet, from the far side of which rises a massive rock. Although there is a recumbent Buddha of great antiquity in the preaching hall, this and all the other images are so crudely painted as to dissipate effectively all their aesthetic value. The little temple on the cliffside, which contains an ancient rock-cut sedent Buddha with modern gilt, is approached by a stairway, and on its left external face it is carved with a beautiful

19. Elephants in relief, Isurumuniya (See page 173)

20. The Aluvihare (See page 175)

Some Buddhist Temples

bas-relief of the god Siva and his wife Parati, dating from the seventh century A.D. They are depicted in a lively and conjugal attitude. While I was inspecting this finely chiselled work my small guide, with a strange lack of perspicacity, informed me that the theme of the scupture was "Grief."

It is, however, in the vicinity of the little tank that the visitor will discover the most important carvings at Isurumuniya. Just above the waterline of the rock is chiselled, in both high and low relief, a group of most spirited, life-size elephants. There are a bull, a cow and a calf standing at the water's edge on one side, and the outlined figure of a fourth elephant with a raised trunk on the other. They are beautifully carved, and their presence lends colour to the legend that they are the guardians of some hidden treasure in the dark green depths below. It is the opinion of the Archaeological Commissioner that these reliefs are the work of Hindu Pallavan artists from southern India, and that they date from the seventh century A.D.

A short distance to the left of the tank, in a niche on the rock, there is an even finer work of sculpture, probably by the same Pallavan artists. It represents a seated man, clearly an ascetic, with his left hand resting on the ground and his other arm supported on his right knee. The visitor will

Ceylon

be deeply impressed by his calm and penetrating eyes, as well as by the skill with which his difficult pose is portrayed. Behind the man is carved a horse's head. According again to the expert authority of the Archaeological Commissioner, this ascetic is the Sage Kapila, and a slight knowledge of his position in Hindu mythology may help the reader to appreciate more fully one of the finest sculptures in Ceylon.

Sagara, King of Ajohhya, had by his Queen Sumati, according to the legends of the *Ramayana*, sixty thousand sons. Her fertility, however, was unluckily not equalled by the piety of her children, who even allowed a horse which their father was about to sacrifice to escape to the nether regions. Whereupon the indignant parent ordered his sixty thousand sons to recover the horse, and they dug down through the earth's surface until they found the complacent animal peacefully grazing in Hades. Unfortunately, on his back was seated in profound meditation the Sage Kapila who, outraged by this interruption, reduced to ashes by the sacred flames that flashed from his eyes King Sagara's sixty thousand unsatisfactory sons. Naturally, after this exploit the Sage Kapila assumed a position of major importance in Hindu mythology, which accounts for his superb portrayal on the rock at Isurumuniya.

Some Buddhist Temples

The visitor will have noticed that this Buddhist temple owes its chief artistic interest to the artists of an alien faith. Originally Singalese, as is attested by the gilded Buddha image on the rock, then in the hands of the Hindus when the Pallavan sculptures were worked, Isurumuniya probably passed back to the Buddhists in the twelfth century, during the reign of King Parakramabahu.

(d) Aluvihare

This remarkable rock monastery is two miles north of Matale, a short distance from the main road. Historically it is of considerable importance, since here in about the year 100 B.C. King Walagambahu, not content with founding Dambulla, convened all the *bhikkhus* of the kingdom of Lanka and ordered them to inscribe on "olas" the Buddhist scriptures, which until that time had been handed down by oral tradition. Originally written in Singalese, these books were translated into Pali in the fifth century A.D., and this later translation is of the greatest value since the Singalese version no longer exists.

The approach to the Vehera is very impressive. Huge rocks on either side form a narrow passage to a delicate belfry, which, even if it is modern, is

Ceylon

certainly of the most appropriate proportions. Another flight of steps leads to a replica of the Buddha's sacred footprint on Adam's Peak, and a very fine view. The temple itself, which on approach lies in the rock on the left, is of little merit, and the garish and even childish pictures which decorate the entrance seem out of place in these grim and dank surroundings. But amongst these great black rocks, hung in the fissures with myriads of bats and towering over the narrow strip of ground which divides them, it seems a safe and fitting place for the *bhikkhus* of Lanka to inscribe, for the first time, the doctrines and discourses of the Buddha. After the lapse of two thousand years one can still visualize them in their yellow and orange robes flitting like saffron and golden butterflies round these Cimmerian rocks.

(e) Gedi-Gé

A breathless walk of one mile from Nalanda through a narrow valley will bring the traveller to a broad fertile plain, shaded at the sides by high trees and backed by distant mountains. In the middle of this plain stand the tall ruins of the Gedi-Gé. Built in granite, now mellowed into a yellow hue, this temple was erected during the

21. The Gedi-Gé

22. *The Preaching Buddha, Aukana Vihara*

Some Buddhist Temples

eleventh century A.D., during the subjection of the island to the Cholas, or Tamils as they are more generally but less accurately called. In style it is of Dravidian origin, and in the elaborate detail of the exterior it resembles the Thuparama and Lankatilaka at Polonnaruwa. But while the two latter temples are of brick, the Gedi-Gé is built of stone. In this respect it is unique in Ceylon, and the chiselling of the stone into the detailed ornaments of the façade must have proved a long and difficult task.

The ruins of this temple, which although Hindu in architecture was built for Buddhist worship, still retain some fine decoration including, in the one remaining gable, the figure of a god with crossed legs. Little dwarf faces make a frieze in round apertures below him. But the great charm of the Gedi-Gé lies in its beautiful colouring and its remote and peaceful surroundings. It reminded me of the ruins of some Cistercian abbey secluded in a lush Yorkshire dale.

(f) *Aukana Vehera*

The object of a visit to this Vehera is to see the great rock-cut Buddha, probably dating from the fifth century A.D., which stands, in even more

Ceylon

romantic surroundings than the Gal-Vihara images at Polonnaruwa, in a remote stretch of jungle near the Kalawewa. Most travellers will probably find time to visit this immense tank built by King Dhatu Sena in A.D. 459, which after many vicissitudes was restored and reopened, to the great benefit of the public, by the British Government in 1888. No fragile visitor should attempt the rather arduous two-mile walk from the tank to the Vehera; an expedition for which a guide is absolutely essential. From the bund of Kalawewa, however, the traveller can pick out in the distant jungle the large rock by which the Buddha stands, and thereby assess his chances of reaching it. On no account should this walk be undertaken during the rains, since not only may the streams on the way prove impassable, but even to be compelled to cross them in a condition of spate, on half-submerged stones or over the uneven surface of a tree trunk, may ruin for many the pleasures of this expedition.

The small compound of the Aukana Vehera contains a Bo-tree, a small modern temple, the great Buddha image, and of course the ubiquitous *bhikkhu*. Unfortunately the Buddha stands at the far end of the compound, and it is necessary to cross its hot and stony surface without shoes or a hat.

Some Buddhist Temples

The latter deprivation is on this occasion rather serious, since if the sun is on the Vehera, which it usually is, it may be necessary for the visitor to curtail his inspection of the image in order to avoid sunstroke. Nevertheless, despite all these difficulties and dangers, indeed perhaps because of them, the first view of this Buddha is unforgettable. He is about fourteen yards high, and from his slightly elevated position he looks across the jungle towards Kalawewa with that supremely disinterested gaze which, although always present in these images, is accentuated by his great stature and commanding situation. A perceptible shadow is thrown over his face by the canopy above his head, but that only serves to increase that air of spiritual detachment inherent in the possession of Buddhahood. Although this figure is considered by experts to be inferior to many in the island from the artistic point of view, yet I am convinced that through the incidence of its size, position and facial expression this image may help the visitor to understand the essential core of Buddhism more than the study of the most erudite books.

Chapter Eight

THE JUNGLE

☼

Here I tread on dangerous ground. I am not a zoologist, an ornithologist nor a horticulturist, and yet, with little knowledge, I greatly loved the Ceylonese jungle. I therefore hope in this cursory description of its beauties that I may entertain, even if I cannot instruct, those readers as interested in the subject as myself. The sumptuous background of trees and flowers should, I think, be described before considering the wild life which lives amongst it, but since I propose to begin with such animals and birds as can normally be seen from the road, I shall omit a description of the wayside scenery, as this is fully discussed in the second part of this book entitled "Pleasant Journeys."

One of the first phenomena which will delight the traveller when he is driving through Ceylon is the number of animals, reptiles and birds which appear to enjoy the tarmac roads, or anyhow their vicinity. Monkeys actually squat on the road in large colonies, perhaps in imitation of the solitary

The Jungle

Singalese or Tamil, who also seems to enjoy its even surface. Perhaps in both cases the reason lies in the comparative absence of insects on tarmac roads, and often when being devoured by ants on their grass edges I have wished that it were safe and dignified to follow their prudent example. These monkeys, whose gay antics are a constant diversion, will either be the smaller brown variety or else the larger grey "Wanderoos." The latter are the more numerous and decorative species, and it is delightful to watch them on the tree-tops, half buried in foliage, chattering with their friends or swinging from bough to bough amongst the sun-dappled branches, but always keeping at a discreet distance from the visitor below. Since he is fortunately never shot for "sport," and nowadays rarely for food, the "Wanderoo" is the most constant and amiable companion.

A less agreeable road user is the ant, of which the traveller will probably encounter three species. There is firstly the white ants, or termites, which build those elaborate golden hills by the roadside. They are a great pest, and nothing can stop their forward march when they are out to destroy. Besides being able to assimilate living plant tissue, which makes them a great menace to the tea plantations, they often attack houses, where they

Ceylon

devour everything except stone and iron. As Knox describes them in his *Historical Relation of Ceylon*: "they creep up the walls of the houses, and build an arch made of dirt over themselves, all the way as they climb, be it ever so high." Less of a menace are the black termites, which live in the ground and are similar to the English variety. The traveller will frequently find them on his person and in his baggage, but fortunately they do not bite. The red termite, on the other hand, has a most savage bite. He lives mostly in trees, where his nest of leaves may be seen hanging by the wayside about the size of a man's hand. These sinister ants will follow a dying animal for miles through the jungle, waiting to devour the flesh and to clean the bones dry. A more amiable and no less industrious insect is the beetle who can often be seen on the road tirelessly pushing in front of him a ball of dung several times larger than himself. I once followed a beetle propelling his hoard up the steps of Mihintale, no doubt in the direction of his hole. Robert the Bruce's spider cannot have provided a more pertinacious or impressive spectacle.

Hares, in colour like the blue hares of Scotland, but with a more edible flesh, dash across the roads by night; but the homely rabbit is unknown in

The Jungle

Ceylon. Squirrels and grey mongoose are often by the wayside during the day. The former, no bigger than the fist of a small child and with his yellow stripes and clockwork motion, might well be more at home in the nursery than in the jungle. The mongoose, a remarkably wary animal, is the greatest enemy of the snake. A snake charmer will stage for the less squeamish visitor a semi-serious battle between a mongoose and a cobra with drawn fangs, separating the combatants as soon as the animal has secured his hold behind the snake's head. But in the jungle the fight is naturally more even, and the mongoose often gets bitten. On these occasions the intelligent animal will sample every herb he encounters, until he finds an antitoxin; but of what this consists is unknown, since the mongoose continues his eager consumption, whether of intent or from ignorance, long after the curative herb has been found.

The least attractive of the larger animals which can often be seen from the road, although usually at dawn and sunset, are the jackals. With similar masks yet with longer legs they are more graceful than the English fox, but they share in common a love of killing and a taste for carrion. The traveller will see them by the road singly or in pairs and, although keeping out of reach of possible danger,

Ceylon

they seem little worried by man. It is, however, at night that the ferocity of these animals is realized, when in great packs they howl through the jungle in search of prey. The smaller deer are often their victims, although the jackal is as well content with the stenching and half-eaten carcass of some larger beast which a leopard has abandoned in disgust some nights before. One evening at Kekirawa I saw a pack of about fifty race past the compound yelling as if possessed by the devil, and although human beings, if healthy and agile, are immune from their attentions, I was glad to be on the right side of the stout barbed-wire fence which surrounded the rest-house. These disgusting animals, which are the terror of all wounded and infirm creatures, can scent the approach of death and often linger expectantly round the hut of a dying man. They have another disagreeable characteristic of emitting such a pungent smell that no man or dog when in their pursuit can approach within forty yards of them, and if killed their carcasses are still protected by this foul odour for some time.

The last animal that is common to the road is the buffalo. Naturally there is the tame variety drawing carts and tilling the fields, but his wild brother can often be seen in open stretches of the

The Jungle

jungle or wallowing in a tank adjacent to a road. This handsome animal may inspire the traveller with an entirely misplaced confidence, for the reason that there is no strict dividing line between a tame and a wild buffalo. When the Ceylonese, for whatever purpose, need the services of these animals a "Kraal" is held to catch them; but when they are no longer required, instead of being kept for the next occasion, they are let loose into the jungle. In consequence, although many buffaloes are entirely wild, none are completely domesticated. A herd of buffalo by the side of a tank are unlikely to prove disagreeable unless they include cows and their calves; but an isolated animal, which may have been evicted from the herd, may easily charge on being disturbed, particularly if the intruder is a European, since a white skin, being less familiar to the animal, is liable to inspire it with a greater anxiety. Having once, out snipe shooting, been chased by a female buffalo who looked as amiable as a milking-cow, I feel entitled to give this advice: every buffalo not in harness should be treated with circumspection by the prudent traveller.

On one occasion, however, I felt more pity for these animals than any I have seen in the jungle. I was motoring on the isolated Bottuwa plains after

Ceylon

leaving the Yala game sanctuary. Here is some of the most beautiful coastal scenery in Ceylon; lagoons separated by undulating duneland and little bays encircled by great red rocks. But it was marred by a strange sight. In a long sea-water lagoon was a herd of about fifty wild buffalo, and when our car drew up by the side they rose to their legs and seemed not unprepared to charge. I noticed, however, that one of the herd remained struggling in the water, clearly unable to rise. Actually the others were exhibiting a spurious courage, since in varying degrees they were all dying from lack of fresh water. Suddenly as they watched us panic overcame them, and they dashed from the lagoon, stumbling slowly and feebly across the sand dunes into the distance. It was tragic to see these magnificent animals in such terrible need. The lack of fresh water before the rains in the Bottuwa plains was admittedly deplorable, but I was assured on good authority that three tanks would soon be available. The future of animal life in that vicinity clearly depended on their construction.

Of the reptiles most often seen from the road is a palagoya, more commonly called the iguana. The presence of those decorative anthills lining the way will be a sure indication of his interest in

The Jungle

the neighbourhood, since the ant is his main and most cherished fare. This thick-tongued member of the lizard tribe usually measures between two and three feet and is defenceless but for his tail, with which he can inflict a disagreeable contusion on his aggressor. His flesh is white and makes most excellent eating, and when Knox was in Ceylon in the seventeenth century there was a superstition that "if you eat other flesh at the same time as you eat of this, and have occasion to vomit, you will never vomit out this, though you vomit all the other." Besides this unexpected advantage from eating the flesh of an iguana, there is a modern superstition investing its tongue with an educational value. Placed raw in a beetle-leaf the tongue is freely given by mothers to their children in the belief that it will develop their intellects. It is, however, no easy task to test the truth of either of these claims made on behalf of the engaging iguana.

Of the birds usually seen from the road the least interesting is the jungle fowl. Excellent to eat, these birds vary little from the domestic variety, and may often be seen scurrying from the roadside into the jungle. Far different is the pleasing and ubiquitous Myna who, although a filthy feeder, is a great ornament to the road with his bright

Ceylon

yellow wattles enlivening the nut brown of his sleek feathers. This bird can easily be tamed, and it will talk with the ease of a parrot. More distinguished is the Golden Oriole, which can frequently be seen from the road flying from tree to tree. His bright yellow body contrasts strangely with his raucous and even offensive cry. The "Seven Sisters" approximate less to the elegant Oriole than to the plebeian Myna. With the colouring of a pale English thrush and a diet exclusively confined to dung, these chattering birds do not belie their appellation in so far as they are always seen in groups of seven. But after only a passing acquaintance with their habits I was reluctant to believe that these birds were all sisters.

The last of the birds usually seen from the road which I have space to mention is perhaps the most delightful of them all: the cheerful Kottoruwa, or Green Barbut. It is a small green parrot with a tufted head and a call, perhaps the most insistent in the island, which resembles a distant foghorn. The Kottoruwa takes a friendly interest in human beings, and I well remember one boiling morning, when I was shooting snipe on a tank near Arugam bay, that one of these spry little birds followed me incessantly, apparently taking a

The Jungle

lively curiosity in the sport. As, however, the latter, as far as I was concerned, was far from satisfactory, I had some difficulty in restraining myself from shooting this pert accompaniment to failure. Unfortunately the Singalese are wont to confine these charming little birds in cages, and the opportunity is often afforded them, since frequently Kottoruwas stun themselves at night against the big lamp always hanging on a rest-house verandah. The Singalese also trap them by placing a bait of food on the trunk of a plantain tree which, being soft, imprisons the beak of the Kottoruwa in the bark. These attractive and harmless little birds deserve better treatment at the hands of men.

The fauna which I have just described are not the only specimens which may be seen from the road, since "rogue" elephants have been known to make most unwelcome appearances on them, while I myself have seen a leopard standing by moonlight on a tarmac road within a mile of the rest-house at Sigiriya. They are, however, those most generally seen, and I now propose to take the traveller from the jungle road into the jungle itself, and first briefly mention the beautiful and luxuriant surroundings in which such a wide variety of creatures live.

A description of the more sophisticated flowers

Ceylon

will be given when the Peradeniya gardens are being discussed, and although it is in the rich tones of green the undergrowth excels, some shrubs and flowers lend colour to the diversity of the jungle. Conspicuous amongst the former is the "Cassia fistula," with yellow bunches of flowers like a giant laburnum, and the "Limonia alata," which for many months of the year is densely covered with a small orange-coloured fruit. More magnificent is the white "Datura fastuosa," resembling a trumpet-shaped lily, while of the bushes of wild hibiscus there is one with white blossoms which in the centre of the bush turns to purple. Shrubs of red poinsettias are fairly common, and there is another variety which mingles white leaves amongst the green. Of the creepers the most beautiful is the "Gloriosa superba," somewhat resembling a honeysuckle in growth. The blossoms are a vivid red and, tongue shaped, they form a cup-like cluster. Other creepers include the luxuriant yellow "Bignonia unguis" and the mauve-pink "Congea." Of the small flowers on the floor of the jungle the most conspicuous are the "Amaryllis," which makes a carpet of bright pink blooms, and the romantic "Four o'clock flower," which is described by Knox with charm and accuracy. "Its nature is to open about four o'clock in the

The Jungle

evening," he wrote, "and so continueth open all night until the morning, when it closeth up itself till four o'clock again. Some will transplant them out of the woods into their gardens to serve them instead of a clock, when it is cloudy that they cannot see the sun." All these flowers, beautiful as they are, only blossom for a short time round the month of March, and it is therefore more instructive to study the trees, which, with or without flowers, are more permanent and distinctive ornaments of the jungle.

Of the flowering trees the most common and striking is the "Flamboyant," which owing to its glaring red flowers is known as "Sore-eye." It grows to a considerable height in a graceful, umbrella-shaped formation. The yellow-flowering tulip tree is also general, and both this tree and the "Flamboyant" flower when other trees are without blossom. Of the trees which flower about March, perhaps the most beautiful are the "Milla," with its yellow bark and pale mauve flowers, and the "Amherstia nobilis," with its sprays of bright coral blooms. Although the ebony tree is more notable for its dark-grey bark, seared with black fissures, and its great domed head, it also produces in March pretty white flowers amongst its bright oval foliage.

Ceylon

Apart from the coconut and the palmyra, discussed in the "Pleasant Journeys," the most noticable tree in the jungle is the banyan. Its trunk, covered with a silvery bark, often assumes the most weird and contorted forms, while its long rope-like arms which hang from the branches often take root in the ground. At Kalutara, for instance, a banyan has formed a huge arch across the main road. The Jak is also a very general tree, easily recognizable by its green-ridged fruit on the trunk. From its bright yellow wood, which with age sobers into a dark brown, the dye is extracted for the orange robes of the *bhikkhus*. The elegant Satinwood tree is fairly common, and although it is generally considered to be an "unlucky" wood, it has the good fortune to be immune from the ravages of the white ant. The traveller will also be attracted by the Kon, or Ceylonese oak, with its hard timber and gay tufts of red leaves. Growing by water the Kumbak tree deserves inspection for its great size and the pink shade of its smooth bark.

Of the lesser trees the Calamander, related to the Ebony, produces the "Zebra" wood which was so popular for English furniture during the late eighteenth and early nineteenth centuries. Nedum, although brittle, is another fine wood for furniture,

23. Leopard at the Kill (See page 196)

24. *The Lower Entrance Gate, Galle (See page 225)*

The Jungle

although its possibilities in this respect have been little explored in Europe. Other useful trees to be found in the jungle include the small Domba, which, with its grey bark, is much in demand for cart-poles; the Keku, with bark which is made into rope; the tall Katuimbul, the timber of which is used for matches; and the Lunumidella, which has so light a wood that it is almost exclusively used for the outriggers of the fishing boats called "Catamarans."

The Ceylonese jungle, however, is not all composed of virgin forests, since many types of fauna inhabit the "Patanas," the open tracts of country spotted with rhododendrons in the hill-country, and the sandy plains, often thick with scrub, which border the sea in different parts of the island. The so-called "park-lands" in the low-country, which usually lie near tanks and were probably once cultivated, are also a favourite resort for the larger animals such as elephants, buffalo and deer. But it is naturally in the jungle covered by the virgin forests that the greatest variety of fauna can be seen, and it is against this rich background, which I have briefly attempted to describe, that I propose to introduce a few of the best-known animals, reptiles and birds.

Of the larger animals which the traveller will

Ceylon

want to see come probably first elephants, leopards, bears, deer, and perhaps wild pig and crocodiles. This is not the place, nor am I the person, to give the natural history of all or any of these animals, but a few general remarks may assist the visitor who, like myself, is not an expert in these affairs. These animals, with the exception of the crocodile, can best be seen at water-holes, preferably situated in a game sanctuary, unless the traveller desires to kill them. A description of water-holes will be given later in this chapter.

It may be helpful to remember this general principle where animals of the above species are concerned: all of them, unless man-eaters, attack through fear, which is engendered by the conviction that escape without fighting is impossible. This generalization naturally includes the case of the wounded animal. Therefore, when disturbed in the jungle they prefer to retreat rather than to attack, with the exceptions of the sloth bear and the tic-polonga, a small and very vicious snake. The elephant, for example, which in Ceylon rarely has tusks and is considered a large beast if over eight feet six inches high, moves away with surprising speed and quiet at the approach of man. The exceptions to this rule are firstly the obvious one of a cow elephant and her calf, and secondly

The Jungle

that of the "rogue" elephant. The latter, which can be shot without a licence, is a general menace owing to his great size and vicious temper. A "rogue" is always by himself, and his savage condition is due to his expulsion from the herd, usually owing to old age, by a younger bull-elephant.

"Rogues" usually frequent the neighbourhood of villages, where food is easily obtainable, and thus can occasionally be encountered on a main road. A few years ago two English sailors had an alarming proof of this habit. They were returning to Trincomalee riding the same motor bicycle, when they suddenly saw a great elephant charging down the road in their pusuit. Owing to a bad surface the sailors were unable to outstrip the animal, which gained on them rapidly. Finding therefore escape by speed impossible, they jumped off the bicycle on reaching a culvert and crept under its welcome protection. Here the elephant obviously could not follow them, and it turned away to inspect the shattered bicycle. Unfortunately the machine was still red-hot from the run, and the "rogue" chanced to burn the tip of his trunk while examining it. Infuriated by this misadventure, he then turned a revengeful attention to the hiding sailors, and collecting rubble in

Ceylon

his trunk he blew it viciously down the culvert with the object of bolting them like ferreted rabbits. The punishment which the young men had to undergo was luckily terminated by the arrival of a motor-omnibus, on which the "rogue" withdrew indignantly into the jungle. Elephants of course live in herds, and the females, being always less precious, undertake the duty of sentinels. Of this custom I once had experience when, on rounding the corner of a jungle path itself made by elephants, I was confronted by a solitary specimen devouring the branches of a large tree less than a hundred yards away. On observing me the animal emitted a shrill cry of warning to the rest of the herd and disappeared into the jungle. She appeared to be almost as alarmed as I was myself.

The leopard is perhaps the most beautiful animal in the jungle, and the one of which its other inmates stand most in awe. Feeding chiefly on deer the leopard is also a menace to monkeys, since on stout trees he can climb with equal agility. In consequence the approach of a leopard is heralded by the wildest chattering in the tree-tops. To watch a leopard at a kill is a great experience since, apart from the feline grace of its movements, the hesitation with which it

The Jungle

approaches the carcass shows the timidity as well as the caution of the animal. I was once privileged from a "hide" to watch a leopard and his "kill," but unfortunately the stench of the latter injuriously affected my mucous membrane, and my consequent ear-splitting sneeze so alarmed the leopard, who was still several yards from his meal, that he bounded into obscurity as if pursued by the devil.

The leopard, in common with other animals, has no desire to molest human beings unless he has discovered at an advanced age that a man is an easier prey than a deer. Once having tasted human flesh and realized the comparative ease of securing it, he becomes a man-eating leopard and an active menace to any native village. I was once given the opportunity of sharing a "hide" with an expert shot anxious to destroy a "man-eater," but when I discovered that the "kill" was the corpse of a man half devoured on the previous evening I declined this courteous but macabre invitation. With the invention of the internal combustion engine, leopards have developed a new sense of fun denied to their less sophisticated ancestors. They are so fascinated by the exhaust of a motor cycle that they will follow it for miles down a jungle road. Their motives are as amiable as those

Ceylon

of a child in pursuit of a toy train, but should the cycle be overtaken the rider might be involved in serious consequences.

The Ceylonese or sloth bear is a disagreeable animal both in habits and appearance. He is usually about five feet high with black mangy fur and a prolonged snout and lips, which enable him to extract honey from rocks and ants from their hills. These with vegetables form his principal diet, but he is not averse to eating carrion as well. The bear has a horrid character and will charge a man at sight and without provocation. He is therefore much feared by the villager, particularly owing to his crafty custom of hiding up a tree and then dropping on the head of the unsuspecting passer-by. He will then, if he is able, bite and claw his victim to death. It is therefore advisable for the traveller carefully to inspect the trees under which he passes in the jungle, especially if he notices their tracks in the vicinity. These can easily be recognized, since the impression made by the hind legs of a bear are practically identical with those of a bare-footed man, except that they are slightly wider across the toes and sharper at the heel. Some of the most alarming noises that the traveller can hear at night in the jungle are the penetrating barks and yells emitted by two bears in congress.

The Jungle

Although deer can sometimes be seen from the road, it is in a game preserve, such as the Yala sanctuary near Tissamaharama, that these beautiful animals can be studied in comfort, since there herds can be encountered which are almost as tame as those in an English park. The spotted deer are the most common, but more unusual to the European is the magnificent dark brown Sambur which sometimes reaches thirty stone in weight and averages five feet in height. The musk or mouse deer is one of the most fascinating but also one of the most timid inhabitants of the jungle. He is little bigger than a rabbit, possessing straight short legs, with little deer hooves and a pointed head like a rat. His tracks resemble holes prodded by a pencil.

Another animal which can be easily seen in a game sanctuary is the wild pig, which however, in my opinion, is an uninteresting beast except on the dinner table. This generality applies in no respect to crocodiles which, although abundant in many tanks and rivers, have become very wary of man owing to the constant efforts made to shoot them on account of the value of their skins. My only personal acquaintance with this carnivorous reptile was at Puttalam on the west coast, where I found one in my vicinity while bathing. Although

Ceylon

it is said that here they are quite harmless to human beings, I preferred instant retreat to testing this amiable reputation of the Puttalam crocodiles. The traveller who is anxious to watch these interesting reptiles should be able to do so, amongst other places, at the Galgamuwa tank half-way between Kekirawa and Puttalam, at the Giant's tank near Vavuniya, on the banks of the Nil-Ganga at Matara, and at the tank at Tissamaharama. It is useless, however, to expect to see a crocodile in a tank just before the rains, when they will all be congregated in the rivers. But the traveller should remember, particularly if snipe-shooting, that the crocodile is able to conceal its capacious maw in very shallow muddy water.

I have already suggested that he who wishes to see the animals just described, with the exception of the crocodile, can best do so by making arrangements to visit one of the recognized water-holes of the jungle. Information on this point is willingly given by the courteous authorities of the Forest Conservancy, by any travel bureau in Colombo, or by the local trackers.

There are an infinite number and variety of tracks which lead to a popular water-hole in the jungle. They are the pilgrim's way of the animal world, to the most vital necessity of their exis-

The Jungle

tence. Far away from the water-holes thin tracks will be found leading into each other and growing ever wider, until at length they combine into a hard beaten track leading straight to water. The most frequented water-holes are those in a natural depression or fissure of the rock, and they are often shaped like a narrow deep canoe, since here water will remain during the long months of drought.

The near vicinity of a water-hole stenches with the droppings of animals, and its edge is often as polished by their feet as is the stone ascent to some Buddhist temple by those of the worshippers. There are usually trees in the vicinity but, where these are absent, it is necessary for the trackers to build so-called "forts" from the loose rock to enable the traveller to watch unseen at the water-hole. Many unsatisfactory nights may be spent in this occupation, but the watcher may while away the long hours of the night by speculating, like Mr. John Still in his delightful book, *The Jungle Tide*, as to what these mysterious dank pools may hold, sunk in their deep mud bottoms. Arrow and spear heads of an earlier civilization would without doubt be discovered; perhaps also drinking vessels and the personal adornments of women, and even the fossil of a prehistoric man. The

Ceylon

secrets both of human and animal activities that one jungle water-hole may preserve in its unplumbed depths, through an unrecorded past to the present day, may one day be revealed by the archaeologist, but until then the animals can drink in peace.

Having described some of the larger animals and their habits, it may be interesting to inquire how the native inhabitants protect themselves from their occasional attacks. I have presumed that the traveller is a student and not a killer of animals, but in any case he can arrange for ample protection in the jungle. This, however, does not apply to the natives, who except under certain circumstances are denied the possession of the gun, which anyhow they would lack the means to buy. They have therefore relied from the most distant times on "Mantharams," and owing to their dislike of killing many would prefer to use them rather than a rifle. These "Mantharams" are traditional incantations which are loudly recited when in danger, with the object of diverting an animal's aggressive intentions by verbal hypnotism. For every beast there is a separate "Mantharam," and the one used on the bear, for instance, is said to close its mouth for forty-five minutes, and with such potency that should another man encounter it during that lapse

The Jungle

of time the bear will be unable to attack him. The snake alone of all fauna is unaffected by "Mantharams," owing to its total deafness. The efficacy of "Mantharams" is well authenticated, and their tradition and execution testify to the latent powers which man can exercise over animals, when unable or unwilling to resort to his superior resources of taking life.

Of the smaller animals which often can be seen in the interior of the jungle the porcupine is as delightful and harmless as any. His wealth of quills makes him appear larger than he really is, and in consequence he has often been shot at a water-hole in mistake for a bear, although he should even be distinguishable at night by the white patch in his rear. In motion, however, there is no mistaking him, since his fifteen-inch quills grate vigorously together and sound like the swirl of taffeta in a mid-Victorian ball-room. His flesh, although rather sickly, is considered a delicacy.

Three other smaller mammals deserve particular mention: the palm-civet, the loris, and the "flying fox." The civet, which although shy can sometimes be observed on his palm-tree, belongs to the cat genus, which he resembles in appearance and character. He is chiefly remarkable for the strong perfume which he secretes in two glands near the

Ceylon

rectum. This perfume is much prized in the East, and therefore the civet is often kept in captivity and his glands are periodically tapped with a spatula. The loris, which belongs to the lemur genus, weighs less than a rat and makes a charming pet. They spend the day asleep on a branch, the body rolled up and the head hidden between the legs. At night they awaken, and their high, eerie cry can be heard from the tree-tops. They resemble humans even more than monkeys, and their pink finger-nails are similar to those of a baby. The "flying fox" belongs to the pestiferous bat tribe, of which sixteen species are known in Ceylon. Most of these resemble in size and habits their European cousins, with the exception of the "Pteropus" or "flying fox," which is of a frugivorous nature and the size and shape of a cat. It may be some time before the traveller will become accustomed to these singular mammals, darkening the pale light of evening with their giant wings. They are certain to remind him of the legendary vampire, but fortunately the "flying fox," unlike some varieties of the bat, does not suck blood.

Of the less reliable inhabitants on the floor of the jungle snakes and leeches take precedence. Amongst the former the hooded snake, or "Cobra de Capello," as it was called by the Portuguese,

The Jungle

is naturally pre-eminent in Ceylon owing to his prevalence and connection with the Buddhist faith. This reptile of course possesses no hood in the literal sense of the word, but by the dilation of his anterior ribs when excited his neck becomes so distended as to produce a hood-like appearance. The cobra, which is usually about five feet long, is a nocturnal feeder on amphibians, birds, reptiles and eggs. He can move rapidly across the ground, whether in attack or retreat, and he can climb and swim with grace and ease. No certain cure is known for his bite, which is of the most poisonous and usually fatal nature, although drugging the victim with spirits and the cauterization of the wound are considered the best remedies. The cobra, however, never bites unless trodden upon or deliberately attacked, and the great beauty of this brave reptile, coupled with his romantic connection with Buddhism, makes him one of the most interesting and respected of the fauna in Ceylon.

A far more dangerous reptile is the tic-polonga, or Russell's viper, which, like the bear, regards instant attack as the best means of defence. But this diminutive viper is comparatively rare in Ceylon, as is also his great contrast in size, the python, which often measures over twenty feet in

Ceylon

length. Should, however, the traveller pass under a tree in which lies concealed a hungry python, little can be done to help him. Passing in an inverse direction from the sublime to the ridiculous, the leech deserves some mention for his remarkable pertinacity in the pursuit of human blood. Any wet patch of grass may produce an abundant crop of the "Haemadispa Ceylonica," as the land-leech is grandiloquently known in the island. He measures about an inch in length and is as thin as a knitting-needle. Unlike the cobra, who is quiescent unless disturbed, the impertinent "Haemadispe" follow in flocks after their intended victim, determined to feast on his blood. If bitten by a leech, it is imprudent to remove the creature by force, as a bad sore will result; rather should salt or the juice of a lemon be applied to his tail. Either will cause instantaneous death.

In concluding this chapter on the jungle, I would like to mention a few birds which I have not included in those seen from the road, nor in those seen on the tanks, which are discussed later in "Pleasant Journeys." The chief game birds are the grey and painted partridge, teal, mallard, quail, peafowl and the Ceylon spur-fowl. These can only be shot from November 1st to May 31st. The snipe, being a migrant, can be shot whenever he

The Jungle

is "in." Green and pink doves abound and make admirable eating, although they hardly come under the category of game birds. Less edible but no less beautiful is the orange-coloured King Crow, a bird connected in legend with the Philosopher's Stone. Eagles are common, and as they are not molested appear to regard with equanimity the presence of man. Often they will fly by the side of a traveller's car on a jungle road, and sometimes perching ahead will watch it pass with fearless staring eyes. Of these the serpent-eagle with his orange-brown body is the most beautiful and ferocious. By the sea he sweeps superbly down on the vilest refuse, and would likewise descend to deprive the dying man or beast of his eyes. Out shooting, the serpent-eagle will often follow you round a tank, waiting for a chance of a free meal of snipe or teal, and sometimes shade your perspiring body from the sun with his wide black wings.

The blue Indian Roller is one of the most colourful birds in the jungle. He has a bluish-green body with a chestnut-brown mantle, and wings and rump of azure blue. The male and female of this nocturnal species have identical feathering, and their name of "roller" is derived from the curious tumbling antics of the male during the breeding season. Another bird which adopts a

Ceylon

curious attitude towards its mate is the hornbill. These bulky frugivorous birds, with their discordant cries and clumsy flight, have large bills surmounted with bony helmets, rendered light by means of numerous air-cells. When the young are hatched the male hornbill instantly incarcerates his wife in her nest in a hollow tree by plastering up the entrance with clay and only leaving a small hole through which he supplies her with food. She is only liberated when the young birds are ready to leave the nest. Of the same species as the hornbill is the hoopoo, although he makes a strong contrast to his awkward cousin with his elegant carriage and black-tipped erectile crest on his tawny head. His body is a delightful blend of buff, black and white feathers, and his name is derived from his sharp call, produced by puffing out the sides of his neck and hammering with his bill on the ground at each note. With less beautiful colouring but with a more harmonious voice is the long-tailed robin, whose song is the most melodious in the jungle. But if this robin has the purest voice, so has the so-called Ceylon bird of paradise the most striking appearance of all. He is actually a brightly hued long-tailed fly-catcher with a forked tail five times larger than his body. The Singalese call him the "cloth-stealer," since owing

The Jungle

to the length of tail he appears to be flying away with a long piece of cloth.

After seeing so many rare and resplendent birds the traveller may be pleased to see two specimens which are very familiar to Europeans. The first is the peacock, by no means rare in Ceylon, which when his feathers are heavy after the rains is hunted by the Singalese with packs of dogs and easily killed. The second is the piebald magpie, a bird of ill-omen in Ceylon as in Europe, for tradition relates that alone of all birds he did not go into full mourning after the Crucifixion.

I have attempted in this chapter to give a description of the more important fauna and flora which the traveller will encounter, if he is fortunate and diligent, in the Ceylonese jungle. His pleasure, however, in this wonderful country will be greatly enhanced if he remembers that for every animal he may see by the roadside or in the forest by day, or by the edge of a water-hole at night, hundreds and perhaps thousands are scrutinizing him with fear and resentment mirrored in their eyes. Man has been for centuries the universal enemy in the jungle, but the individual traveller can always try not to increase that enmity by the callous persecution or fruitless destruction of animal life.

PLEASANT JOURNEYS

☼

A—*Colombo. Thence to Mount Lavinia, Kalutara, Galle, Matara, Tangalla, Hambantota, Wellawaya, Pottuvil, Batticaloa, Kalkuda and Trincomalee*

I now propose to accompany the enthusiastic reader on five separate journeys, by road, through Ceylon. I have chosen the motor rather than the more picturesque bullock-cart as a means of conveyance since in the latter, moving at the normal pace of two miles an hour, it would take several years of unbroken travel to cover the different routes I have selected. I have also spurned the railways; firstly because most visitors to the island usually favour a motor or motor-coach and, secondly, because I myself never travelled in a train in Ceylon. I am told, however, that this was a mistake on my part.

These five journeys naturally cannot include all the roads in the island, but they cover the greater majority and also all the most important towns and centres of scenic or historical interest. My point of

Ceylon

departure for each journey is arbitrary, and it will be sometimes necessary to retrace our steps, since the lack of roads often prevent circular excursions. As the visitor from all parts of the world, with the exception of India, is compelled to land at Colombo, I am taking that city as our first starting-point, and I must briefly describe it before taking the road south to Galle.

The derivation of the name "Colombo" is obscure and possibly uninteresting, but at least it has no connection with that of the discoverer of America. Probably the name is either a combination of two native words, "Cola" meaning a leaf, and "Ambo" a mango fruit, or more simply it may be derived from "Columba," the dove. In neither case is it clear why Colombo should have been called after a tree or a bird, and the Dutch, with their tidy minds, attempted to settle the rival theories by giving the city a coat-of-arms combining the mango-tree and the dove.

Before the advent of the Portuguese in the sixteenth century, Colombo had only been a small town protected by a stockade, since Galle in the south was the port of call and, indeed, retained that position for another three hundred and fifty years. In 1550, however, the Portuguese fortified Colombo and, a century later, the circumference

Pleasant Journeys

of these grey stone ramparts was increased to a mile. The native town or "Pettah" was left outside, and it is interesting to note that the designations, the "Fort" and the "Pettah," are still used when referring to the European and commercial area as opposed to the native quarter. Early in the nineteenth century, when Ceylon was seized by Great Britain, the fortifications were enlarged in order to accommodate seven batteries and thirty pieces of heavy cannon, but fifty years later the forts becoming obsolete and the dangers of foreign invasion being remote, it was decided to convert Colombo into the principal port of the island in the place of Galle. In 1875 the Prince of Wales laid the foundation stone of the first breakwater of the Colombo harbour works, and other breakwaters were erected in the following twenty-five years at the approximate cost of one and a half million pounds. The harbour now encloses an area of six hundred and fifty acres.

Colombo to-day may be roughly divided into three distinct quarters: the Fort, the Pettah, and the large residential area known as Cinnamon Gardens. This definition excludes such suburbs as Colpetty and Bambalapitiya, which extend for several miles south of the city. The Fort is as noisy and crowded as any city in Europe, and its histori-

Ceylon

cal remains are rather disappointing. The old Fort Church attracts some attention and lies near the Grand Oriental Hotel, which for practical purposes is usually considered the centre of the Fort area. This church, which originally formed a part of the residence of the Dutch Governors, is a bleak erection containing some inoffensive memorials and a very fine set of silver-gilt altar furniture presented by George IV. These beautiful ornaments are fully representative of the late Regency period. Although otherwise unimportant, a certain humorous interest is attached to this church since, when the English first occupied Colombo in 1796, it was used as a court of law during the day, as a ball-room at night, while on Sundays it was hallowed by the recital of the Book of Common Prayer.

The Grand Oriental Hotel nearby is not only, together with the Galle-Face Hotel outside the Fort, one of the best-known and most comfortable hotels in the East, but it is also a building of some historical renown. To the right of the entrance the visitor will observe a stone recording the facts that "In the reign of King William IV, this Barrack . . . for which £30,000 was granted by His Majesty's Govt. in 1835, was commenced on the 23rd February, 1837, and was completed on the

Pleasant Journeys

27th October, 1837, when the Rt. Hon. Sir Robert Wilmot Horton, Bart., G.C.H., was Governor of the island . . ." Although disappointing to the visitor, it is fortunate for the guests of the G.O.H., as it is always called, that the appearance of this building has changed out of all recognition since those early days.

Besides the old Fort Church, the only other antique church of note in Colombo is the Wolfenhal Church in the Pettah. In it the rites of the Dutch Reformed Church are still performed, but at other times it is always closed. This church was erected by the Dutch late in the seventeenth century, and it contains an ornate font supported by three bulbous legs, typical of that period in Holland. The pulpit is in the same massive style, but there are some pleasant chairs dating from the middle of the eighteenth century and made from the ebony and calamander woods in the island, which some may consider to be the most distinctive ornaments of this gaunt edifice.

By far the most attractive building in Colombo is the Queen's House, the residence of the Governor. That to-day it still rejoices in the name, although three kings have ruled and gone since the end of Queen Victoria's auspicious reign, may perhaps

Ceylon

be regarded as a tribute either to the prophetic powers or to the innate conservatism of the British people. The house is white and rambling, dignified but not pretentious, with a charming garden facing the sea. Although originally built by the Dutch in the eighteenth century, it has been considerably altered and enlarged by successive English Governors, and to-day, with its kindly and inconsequent façade cut up by irregular fenestration and roof-levels, Queen's House is typical of the more benevolent and less rapacious aspects of the British Raj in Ceylon.

I now propose to take the reader along the beautiful south-west and south coast, a distance of seventy-two miles, to the fascinating town of Galle, Colombo's one-time rival and predecessor as the first port in the island. We have not, however, quite finished with Colombo, since after passing the Clock Tower, which with rare adaptability also serves as a lighthouse, the road emerges on to the Galle-Face Esplanade, and immediately on the left rises the massive pile of the State Council. The buildings which house it were finished about fifteen years ago and follow the classical style of architecture. They are well worth a visit, for which permission can be easily obtained. With its broad flight of approaching steps and the high

Pleasant Journeys

pediment surmounting the Royal Arms, the State Council is an imposing if unimaginative erection, gazing with some natural hesitation across the pale green wastes of the Indian Ocean. The interior is commodious, and there is a delightful pillared hall in which members of the Council can, and indeed do, entertain their friends to tea. The Council itself is housed in a lofty and well-aired chamber and, in order to avoid any undesirable controversy, I will content myself by remarking that the public galleries are far better placed, from the point of view of hearing and seeing, than those in the English Houses of Parliament. It is very pleasant for the visitor to watch the colourful occupants of these comfortable galleries as they gaze with awe and admiration on the birth-pangs of democracy in Ceylon.

On leaving the State Council and continuing left down a long stretch of sandy grass bordering the sea, the eye is blinded by the glaring red façade of the Galle-Face Hotel, or G.F.H. as it is more familiarly called. At one time this dreary expanse was mitigated by the presence of a group of trees near the hotel, but some years ago complaints were made by guests of the disturbing cries emitted by the large number of crows which were harboured by these trees. Since it was impossible for

Ceylon

the authorities as Buddhists to exterminate a proportion of these raucous birds, it was decided to cut down all the trees. This intemperate action, however, has in no way discouraged the crows, which still cover the hotel like a black cloud and, in their search for delicacies, often penetrate into the bedrooms of the guests.

Having passed the G.F.H., the Cinnamon Gardens lie to the left of the road to Mount Lavinia. Here live in elegant seclusion the rich of all races in Colombo. Their houses are undistinguished in construction but enviable for the floral and arboreal surroundings. The Colombo Museum is in this neighbourhood, and it contains a magnificent collection of bronzes and ivories relating to Buddhist art. The curious may be interested in the hideous masks of the devil-dancers, as also in the throne and regalia of the last King of Kandy, who was deposed by the English in 1816. These ponderous and inartistic objects had reposed for more than a century in Windsor Castle, when they were returned to Ceylon by King George V. For those who prefer animals to art there is a large collection of stuffed fauna on the first floor.

The eight-mile road from Colombo to Mount Lavinia is mainly covered by suburbs, although in Bambalapitiya an interesting church in the Baroque

Pleasant Journeys

style is passed, which was built by the Portuguese early in the seventeenth century. This gay architectural construction, so clearly designed for Catholic ritual, was converted by the Dutch into a conventicle for their austere and reformed faith. It is now used as an Anglican Parish Church.

The interest and charm of Mount Lavinia are centred in the hotel which projects into the sea from a high rocky plateau. The original house was built in 1824, and it was intended to be the residence of the Governor. As soon, however, as the building was completed the authorities decided that it was too far distant from Colombo. After a short period of neglect the house was adapted to its present use. The beautiful name of Lavinia was that of the wife of Sir Edward Barnes, the Governor.

There is nothing to see at Mount Lavinia except a delightful aquarium, and nothing to do except to bathe, which can be done within the wide reef of coral in comparative safety for Ceylon. Outside, backwash, currents, and sharks abound. For the early riser, however (and all wise travellers should be in Ceylon), there can be few greater pleasures than to witness the fishing fleet of sailing canoes going to sea at sunrise. "Catamarans" they are universally although, I believe, incorrectly called.

Ceylon

They are hollowed out of a tree-trunk, and rising high out of the water they are perilous to manipulate for an inexperienced hand. A "Catamaran" is propelled by bright brown sails, and it is steadied by an outrigger which is attached to the canoe by thick cords of coir rope made from the fibre of the coconut. I have been told that rarely if ever are these boats constructed with iron, since the Loadstone Mountain is thought by the Ceylonese to raise its magnetic head somewhere in the Indian Ocean, and to draw all iron objects irresistibly towards it. There is usually a swell in these seas, particularly during the monsoons, often hiding the frail canoes from the sight of land. At dawn a fleet of "Catamarans," rising on the silver waves which the sun has flicked with aquamarine, appear like a cloud of brown butterflies intent on a distant and hazardous migration.

Reluctantly abandoning the pleasures of Mount Lavinia, the traveller must now take the road due south to Kalutara. To his right a short fringe of sand, covered with white coral and pink quartz, is overhung by lolling coconuts, spreading at random their green and golden leaves like the feathers of some exotic bird. It is entirely coconut country, broken by small villages every few miles. This is tame and domestic scenery.

Pleasant Journeys

Kalutara, which is nineteen miles from Mount Lavinia, can boast a small Dutch fort of the seventeenth century and many pleasant houses of the same period, since during the Dutch occupation it enjoyed a social reputation and drew to its peaceful shores the wealthy burghers from Colombo. The rest-house here is excellent, but there is little need for the traveller to linger, unless he is a lover of strange hats woven from grass fibres and dyed red and yellow. This industry, together with fishing, forms the principal occupation of the inhabitants of Kalutara. Thirteen miles south lies Bentota, with its beautifully situated rest-house at the mouth of the Gin-Ganga. It is fashionable with Europeans from Colombo, and therefore to dally on its palm-shaded shores is a matter for individual taste.

The fifteen miles that separate Bentota from Ambalangoda pass through similar coconut country, with the tempting shark-infested sea a few yards from the road. Lagoons, however, are now frequent and picturesque, and many are ornamented with that curious vegetation the mangrove. This tree thrives exclusively at the mouths of tidal rivers, where it can be washed by salt water. Large seedlings hang from its branches, and from the lower stem protrude tangled roots supporting the mangrove like a pair of stilts. Perhaps it was

Ceylon

from this strange arboreal phenomenon that the fisher folk derived their idea of fishing from stationary stilts in the shallow waters of the sea, often as much as a hundred yards from the shore. In any case, one of the most delightful visions along this lovely coast are the slender forms of the stripped fishermen swaying on their tall stilts against the background of a fiercely setting sun.

The mangrove has another peculiarity which can be studied by the traveller with time and patience at his command. On its roots, when the tide goes down, the "climbing fish" can sometimes be seen making his uneasy way. He is a humble and undistinguished little creature, but he is classified as a fish and I have seen him climb a tree. He has, however, a rival in the "walking fish" which inhabit the northern part of Ceylon. These fish walk briskly from one tank to the other during the rainy seasons. There are even to be found in this astonishing island fish which sing, but I will postpone discussion on these finned musicians until our visit to their domicile—Batticaloa.

There is nothing to detain the traveller at Ambalangoda which, as has been said, is fifteen miles south of Bentota, except a pleasant rest-house and a pretty natural rock bath within a coral reef, which is reported to exclude sharks from the

25. The "Star" Fort, Matara (See page 226)

26. *Elephants bathing in the Nil-Ganga* (See page 227)

Pleasant Journeys

vicinity of the shore. A further twenty miles along the coast road, through coconut plantations and a village called Hikkaduwa, brings the traveller to Galle.

This town is perhaps the most attractive in the south of the island, and it is justly renowned for the large and picturesque Dutch fort, built in the middle of the seventeenth century. As you approach it from the north, the massive grey walls give the impression of guarding some immense prison, and it is a surprise to find on driving through the portcullis that the principal part of the town is housed in the fort to-day. There are only two entrances, and the one which leads to the shore is finely embellished with the Dutch arms—a cock surmounting a shell above the letters "V.O.C.," the initials of the United East India Company. The only other object of intrinsic merit in Galle is the church, usually locked, situated by the hotel. Guide-books normally refer to it as "this fine old Dutch Church," and although the first two adjectives are undoubtedly correct, it is only Dutch *de facto* rather than *de jure* since the church was built, probably towards the close of the sixteenth century, by the Portuguese. The interior, however, with its arid, whitewashed walls is certainly reminiscent of the treatment suffered

Ceylon

by Catholic churches in Holland during the Reformation. But Galle is altogether delightful, with a reasonable hotel and bathing reputed to be safe, while it is permeated with a seventeenth-century atmosphere which any town in Europe would be proud to possess.

We have now covered the seventy-two miles from Colombo to Galle, and although it is more usual for the average traveller to retrace his steps, I am presupposing that he has time at his disposal and is eager to continue the journey along the south coast to Matara, Tangalla and Hambantota. He must then traverse an irregular and inevitable triangle into the interior, eventually to arrive at Pottuvil on the east coast. Thence I propose to conduct the indefatigable traveller, due north along the coast, through Batticaloa and Kalkuda Bay until we arrive at that naval oasis, Trincomalee.

The road from Galle to Matara, a distance of twenty-seven miles, continues to run by the sea and the country maintains the same prosperous and cultivated appearance, either coconuts or fishing being the chief means of livelihood of the people. Matara possesses two Dutch forts; the larger, by the sea, containing the Government buildings and an excellent rest-house; while the smaller, called the "Star" fort, is situated on the

Pleasant Journeys

northern outskirts of the town. The latter, in my opinion, is by far the most beautiful fort in Ceylon, and it has the unique charm of being built of white coral. It is therefore free of that austere aspect inevitable when grey stone is used. As its name implies, this fort is constructed in the shape of a star, and it is entered by a picturesque gateway ornamented with the initials "V.O.C." as at Galle, and the arms of the Governor Van Eck who built it in 1763. The Star Fort is surrounded by a copse of high trees, and the sun pouring through their branches flecks the mottled coral into a score of soft shades. Indeed, when I passed it one hot afternoon in September it reminded me of some fabulous palace conceived by Dulac out of which a fairy prince might at any moment emerge. Matara is situated on the Nil-Ganga (Blue River), a broad and most inviting stream, but unfortunately inhabited by the most ferocious alligators.

Matara is the most southernly town in Ceylon and Dondra Head, which is five miles eastwards off the main road, is the last piece of land between the island and the South Pole. The lighthouse at Dondra towers above deep rock pools, which are filled with a variety of brilliant sea anemones and jellyfish. Iridescent in their beauty, these enemies of bathers can here be inspected in safety.

Ceylon

Returning to the main road after this educational digression, Tangalla is reached after a stretch of eighteen miles of undulating and sandy country. Cultivation and coconuts become rare, since we are gradually approaching the south-east jungle area. The rest-house at Tangalla is a charming eighteenth-century Dutch building with a wall that is washed by the sea. The town, which is undistinguished, is situated round the edge of a pleasant bay.

After a further twenty-six miles through similar coastal country Hambantota is reached. The small bay here is one of the most beautiful in Ceylon, and as the rest-house is excellent and the bathing comparatively safe Hambantota is an admirable place at which to break one's journey. The town is picturesque, but being larger it is therefore noisier than many, and the neighbourhood of the rest-house, which is on the outskirts, is the more peaceful area. From the verandah of this spacious and comfortable building, which lies about sixty feet above the sea, the visitor can gaze across a narrow bay, which is about three hundred yards wide in the town and a similar width at the ingress of the sea nearly a mile away. Below the verandah grow yellow tulip trees stretching down to the hard golden beach, which is broken by emerald-

Pleasant Journeys

green rocks washed by the white rollers of an aquamarine ocean. The beach on the town side is covered with a rhythmic row of brown "Catamarans" with yellow sails all hoisted as if at sea. The jungle extends to the eastern horizon, a discoloured dun-green in the midday sun. Across its uneven surface stretch the disjointed blue hills of Kataragama, which appear like a herd of Brobdingnagian elephants returning to the jungle from the sea.

Leaving Hambantota, I hope with regret, the traveller takes the north-east road which leads to Wirawila, a distance of fifteen miles. The country now changes completely and, instead of the cultivated and undulating scenery of the coast, the road passes through low, scrubby trees surrounded by expanses of bleak sand. Rather curiously, in my inexperienced opinion, this arid waste was considered suitable by the authorities for a bird sanctuary and, possibly by chance, I rarely drove along a road in Ceylon from which so few birds could be seen. Close to Wirawila lies Tissamaharama, surrounded by some of the most attractive country in the island. Tissa itself has been discussed with the "Lost Cities," while the country around was mentioned in the chapter on the jungle, but the traveller should remember that at this point in his

Ceylon

journeys he can visit the Yala game sanctuary and the remains at Tissamaharama. We will therefore take the road due north from Wirawila to Wellawaya, a distance of forty miles.

The jungle along this road is, in my judgment, as interesting as any in Ceylon. At first, however, the vegetation gainsays a jungle: it is almost English in its domestic flavour. At any moment you feel that a cock pheasant or a startled rabbit may cross the road, and it is difficult to believe that this is virgin forest infested with large and unfriendly animals. But this impression of England will quickly fade when you see a golden eagle on an adjacent tree gazing at you with inquisitive but fearless eyes, when green parrots screech over the car and grey monkeys bound from the road to let you pass. Then gradually the jungle changes. The undergrowth becomes thicker, and the short trees give way to high and austere banyans, their rope-like feelers interlaced with parasite and liana. Sometimes these creepers spread to the summit of the banyans and, intertwining from tree to tree, make on both sides of the road a sinister background of impenetrable green. There are few birds, but the air is rent by the ceaseless scream of the tree-beetle. There is nowhere in Ceylon that I have felt a keener sense of solitude.

Pleasant Journeys

As Wellawaya is approached the jungle becomes more friendly and the trees less tall and sinister. Just before a monsoon, clouds of white butterflies with pale green underwings may be seen floating down the road in search of water. When I passed along this road in September it was alive with iguanas. I counted over eighty in the last five miles to Wellawaya, and then I became tired of counting. These vast, cumbersome lizards were feasting on the ants in their turreted gold hillocks. I have to admit to my shame that on this occasion I shot a few of these amiable creatures, but I was hungry, and boiled slices of iguana make a delicious meal. Nemesis, however, overwhelmed me at the rest-house, where I proposed to stay, since the "boy" there, being a Buddhist, declined to cook the iguanas for my dinner.

Wellawaya is rather a squalid little town with a definitely "up-country" atmosphere. It is situated at the foot of the mountains, and here the jungle once more gives way to cultivation and the coconut. There is no need to linger at Wellawaya, unless for refreshment at the rest-house, and we will take the eastern road which, after passing through Buttala and Monargalla, will bring us to Pottuvil on the east coast of the island. As far as Monargalla the road undulates through coconut

Ceylon

plantations at the foot of the hills; then with relief we return to the jungle. Of this stretch of road, from Monargalla to Pottuvil, I have unfortunately little recollection, since I was comatose through a surfeit of curry prepared by the admirable rest-house keeper at the former town. I do, however, dimly remember a great variety of birds along this road, of which the green parrot seemed to predominate.

The east coast of Ceylon is, in my opinion, the most attractive part of the island, and the traveller who proposes to stay in the neighbourhood of Pottuvil should make Arugam Bay his headquarters. The excellent rest-house there lies a few miles south of Pottuvil and is quite isolated by the shore, in a clearing cut out of the jungle. It is as remote as any rest-house in Ceylon, being unencumbered by a village and only connected with the south by a rough and narrow road. A hundred yards from the shore a magnificent, and for bathers a suicidal, sea is broken by a long coral reef into great white rollers, but except for their ceaseless reverberation Arugam Bay is an oasis of great peace and solitude.

A few hundred yards north of the rest-house lies the Arugam Tank, a vast reservoir built by a king of the Greater Dynasty. Its blue waters are

27. The Fort, Batticaloa (See page 234)

28. "Snake-birds" (See page 259)

Pleasant Journeys

usually covered with a concourse of white cranes, black cormorants and the parti-coloured "Mango" birds, while the reeded fringes of the tank are shared by the whistling snipe and the uncertain buffalo. For those who, like myself, enjoy quiet blood sports, the snipe-shooting here is excellent, and from December to April the tank is alive with duck and teal.

Even in memory I would love to linger at Arugam Bay, but rather must I now dislodge the reluctant traveller from its tranquil reaches and accompany him on the road due north to Batticaloa, which is sixty-five miles away. Many regard this coast road as uninteresting, but for me there is infinite charm in the remote villages and scrubby jungle which are passed on the way, with the green, turgid sea on the right, sometimes almost washing the road and a little later fading from sight. If there is time, a stop should certainly be made at Kalmunai, forty miles from Pottuvil, where an excellent and isolated rest-house stands on a deserted foreshore, as at Arugam Bay. This place is deeply engraved on my memory, since on arriving there late for luncheon, my car sank four feet into a treacherous stretch of sand, from which it was only extricated after three hours of exhausting labour. As the car was being excavated

Ceylon

under the pitiless rays of a midday sun, I was compelled to curtail my activities to offering good advice to a number of enthusiastic and semi-nude helpers. One of these I recollect in particular: he was only wearing the *sarong*, or native skirt, and penetrating with difficulty his hairy chest, I distinguished the Royal Arms of Great Britain tattooed upon it, with a cobra "rampant" on either side.

The country between Kalmunai and Batticaloa, a distance of twenty-five miles, changes little in general aspect, but the almost complete absence of cars on this road can be very remarkable. The only private car I encountered on the whole stretch from Pottuvil to Batticaloa belonged to a Judge who was lunching at Kalmunai. But solitude, however refreshing, eventually becomes a burden, and perhaps it will be a relief to arrive at the large and interesting town of Batticaloa.

The capital of the Central Province and a region of coconut and paddy cultivation, Batticaloa is chiefly occupied by Tamils who have little contact with Europeans. The inhabitants are therefore picturesque if inquisitive, and fortunately Western dress is rarely seen. The main charm of Batticaloa, apart from its impressive rest-house, is the large and rambling fort which stretches for miles along the beautiful lagoon. Originally built by the Portu-

Pleasant Journeys

guese at the end of the sixteenth century, it was considerably enlarged by the Dutch after they had captured it in 1639.

For many, however, the great interest of Batticaloa will not lie in the fort, since almost similar erections can be seen elsewhere, but in the "singing" fish which inhabit the depths of the lagoon. Personally I felt rather sceptical as to what I might hear when, at 10.30 p.m., I was being rowed across the dark expanse of the waters by two sturdy Tamils in a high and precarious canoe. But on reaching a certain point the boat was allowed to drift, and sure enough the music of the "singing" fish could be distinctly heard below. It reminded me of the "twanging" in thirds of the "g" string on the violin; but sometimes a single high note with the quality of the "e" string was "sung," out of harmony and sequence with the persistent and monotonous cadence of the *leit motiv*. It was a most uncanny and indeed unmusical sound, but it certainly emanated from under the water. I was told locally that this noise was either emitted by molluscs in congress, or else by crabs scratching each other's backs. I cannot, however, vouch for either of these lively explanations of a phenomenon which, I believe, still baffles the experts. Returning across the lagoon after this

Ceylon

startling experience, I was delighted by the iridescent beauty of the water under the cruel white of the moon. It was a breathless evening, and from the lights on shore the still surface of the lagoon was broken with painted shafts of fire.

If the traveller is not careful, he will be shown, either at Batticaloa or in the neighbourhood, a man or a woman purporting to belong to the "Veddahs," the original and now expiring tribe which exclusively inhabited Ceylon before the arrival of the Singalese. These people, who live in caves or in hollow trees and feed principally on wild honey, undoubtedly still exist to-day; but the isolated specimen produced for the edification of the casual visitor is rarely, if ever, a genuine "Veddah." I well remember, when shooting near Batticaloa, being confronted by an unappetizing individual who clearly hoped to deceive me. Although he was practically naked and emitted fierce guttural cries in my direction, I was convinced that he was no more a "Veddah" than myself. My assumption proved correct since, on being rebuffed, he resumed his *sarong* and singlet and moved disconsolately away.

Avoiding "Veddahs" as far as possible, we now take the road to Trincomalee, a distance of eighty-three miles, although the traveller would be well

Pleasant Journeys

advised to stay at Kalkuda rest-house, which is seventeen miles north of Batticaloa and three miles east off the main road from Valaichchenai. The deserted country along this short stretch of road consists of scrubby jungle and expanses of sand pitted with small lagoons, which from April to November provide excellent snipe-shooting. Together with Arugam Bay and Kekirawa, a village in the centre of the island which we shall visit on another "Pleasant Journey," I have more lively and tender memories of Kalkuda than of anywhere else in Ceylon. I cannot attempt to explain the specific reason for such sentiments, since all these three places can be matched, or even surpassed, in beauty by others in the island. But the general cause may lie in the frequent incidence that profound emotional reactions usually result from undefined and unforeseen circumstances, while mental preparations for an expected and overwhelming emotion may subconsciously defeat the object in view.

The village of Kalkuda consists of a few ordinary boutiques and a long, low rest-house, under the control of a most competent host. It is backed by the jungle, fringed with sand, and lies a hundred yards from the sea. The way across the beach is through an uneven pattern of high palmyras, and

Ceylon

the sands shelve suddenly as the water is reached; yet the bathing is safe for those who can swim. I well remember bathing from this fascinating rest-house one evening in October. The rains had just begun; dark sapphire-blue thunderclouds were gathering over us from inland, towards the horizon the sky was the colour of a pale aquamarine. As we left the warm, turgid water large rain-drops began to fall, hissing as they struck the quivering leaves of the sun-baked palms.

Those who are wise or fortunate enough to linger at Kalkuda should visit the Vakaneri tank, twelve miles south-west of the village. A track, passable for a motor, leads to within a quarter of a mile, and when I approached this placid stretch of water, one bright October sunrise, it presented to my eyes one of the fairest sights I had ever seen. The tank was not full, but two large and irregular expanses were completely covered with white and black birds. It seemed as if there was not enough bright blue water to accommodate such a vast throng. Cranes predominated, as large as swans, and made distinct patterns with the jet-black cormorants, while flocks of pelicans lazily stretched their tousled wings in the yellow herbage at the waterside. It was a spectacle of great beauty, and it appeared in retrospect a boorish action, by

Pleasant Journeys

shooting some confiding snipe, to disturb such a radiant multitude. Yet in part I was rewarded, since at my shot the birds rose into the air like two conflicting stormclouds, and the whirring of their wings resounded like thunder.

The sixty-six miles between Kalkuda and Trincomalee are lengthened, although variegated, by seven ferries and, since portions of the road are often inundated during the rainy seasons, it is advisable to make inquiries from the police before embarking on this somewhat hazardous route. It is difficult to suggest even an approximate length of time necessary to cover these sixty-six miles, since the rivers vary in width and in strength of current, and if the ferry-boat chances to be on the opposite side of the river to yourself, an hour or more may pass before the return journey is made. Communication with the District Engineers at either Trincomalee or Batticaloa, according to the point of departure, asking the official concerned to arrange for the boats to be on the near sides of the rivers, may or may not facilitate the journey. If stranded, however, for any length of time, it is consoling for the traveller to know that there are adequate rest-houses at Valaichchenai, Panichchankeni, Katiraveli, Koddiyar, and an admirable one at Mutur.

Ceylon

The ferry-boat itself is a most picturesque if primitive craft, and it is either punted or paddled by two or more coolies. The close proximity of bullock-cart and motor is agreeable, and a crowd of colourful people, either crouching on or around the car, or weighing down one side of the ferry at the expense of the other, increases the interest of the passage. Sixty cents is charged, irrespective of the distance or the size of the boat, and a large notice repudiating all Governmental responsibility ornaments every landing-stage. It would be difficult to imagine a more appropriate undertaking for Government control.

Despite these difficulties, it is to be hoped that travellers will not be discouraged from using this attractive and eventful road from Batticaloa to Trincomalee. The country is divided between coconut plantations, stretches of open sand and some fine jungle. An additional pleasure in this region is the almost complete absence of motor traffic, and the number of animals and birds which in consequence throng the road. Monkeys in great profusion seem especially to favour this country, the birds of the jungle appear tamer than elsewhere, while I personally encountered such immense clouds of white butterflies along this route that it was necessary to slow down to

Pleasant Journeys

ten miles an hour in order to avoid a possible accident.

Few travellers in the past used to go to Trincomalee, but now that there is a first-class hotel, outside the town and beautifully situated above the harbour, Trincomalee can be used as a luxurious centre for various excursions in the northern and central provinces of the island. The town is of no interest except for Fort Frederick which, although disfigured by a tennis court, is a pretty area inhabited by spotted deer. At the extreme end of the fort rises Swami Rock, four hundred feet above the sea, where once there stood a great temple dedicated to the goddess Siva, which was destroyed from religious motives by the Portuguese. Nevertheless the place is still venerated by the Tamils, and on occasions gaily dressed Hindu ladies process to the heights of Swami Rock and cast floral offerings into the sea. Of less interest is the story of a Dutch girl called Francina van Rhede, who in the seventeenth century cast herself from this rock in a fit of amorous despair.

Excellent deep-sea fishing can be had at Trincomalee, and bathing can be enjoyed by those who accept the verdict of the inhabitants that the sharks in the bay are not man-eaters. But the north-east

Ceylon

monsoon in October is accompanied by a multitude of luminous jelly-fish, and only a robot can contemplate bathing in such colourful yet insidious company.

This is the end of our first "Pleasant Journey."

PLEASANT JOURNEYS

☼

B—*Trincomalee to Horawapotana, Vavuniya, Mankulam, Mullaittivu, and Jaffna: returning via Mankulam, Vavuniya, and Madawachchiya to Mannar; Madawachchiya to Anuradhapura, Mihintale, and Trincomalee*

One mile outside Trincomalee the traveller is once again in a jungle, which cannot be surpassed in beauty and interest by any in Ceylon. Some of the road is bordered by magnificent forest, and the summits of the giant banyans almost touch, to form a spacious tunnel of silvery green. Wild animals of all descriptions inhabit this jungle, and at dawn and sunset nowhere are jackals more likely to be seen from the road. These alert but foul-feeding creatures, usually encountered in twos or threes, show more curiosity than fear of the passing car. The unwelcome bear also favours the neighbourhood and omnibus drivers, who always carry a gun, are rewarded by the authorities with seven rupees and fifty cents for every bear delivered at the police station.

Ceylon

The hot springs at Kanniyai lie five miles from Trincomalee and half a mile from the road through thick jungle. It is advisable to be provided with a guide in order to reach them in comfort and safety. These springs are enclosed by a wall, and each emerges hot and bubbling into a separate basin. They are named after Kannya, the virgin mother of King Ravana, a mythical monarch to whom Vishnu appeared at this place.

Horawapotana is the first large village to be reached. It is thirty-three miles from Trincomalee, and here the journey can be most pleasantly broken. The rest-house is excellent and situated by an attractive tank, alive with cormorants and cranes. Here in October I was fortunate enough to see a quantity of kingfishers feeding below the bund. It was delightful to watch these vivid blue birds perched around on the dark rocks, many with quivering silver fish in their small tenacious bills.

At Horawapotana the right-hand road must be taken to Vavuniya, thirty miles away. This is a most remote and adventuresome route. Human beings are very scarce, and the animals and birds seem tame and inquisitive in the dense jungle on either side. The surface of the road, however, is uncertain, being constructed of sand; and after

Pleasant Journeys

rain it would be difficult to find any substance on which it is easier to skid. At Vavuniya the main Anuradhapura-Jaffna road is joined, and another twenty-eight miles bring the traveller to Mankulam, where the rest-house keeper once prepared for the author a most memorable curry.

The country through which the visitor is now passing is part of the "Vanni," once a most prosperous and thickly populated district which is now covered with the densest jungle. Efforts are being made by the rural authorities to restore the irrigation works, probably constructed over two thousand years ago, and to improve in general the conditions of life in this rather unhealthy country. But the Tamil of the "Vanni," I have been assured, lacks the enterprise and industry of his Jaffna brother, and his marked antipathy to either mental or bodily exertion somewhat impedes the great work of reconstruction in this area. The "Vanni," however, provides a magnificent jungle, which personally I shall always connect with birds and trees rather than with animals, although the latter exist there in great numbers. The tall satinwood trees of the "Vanni" fascinated me, as did the lean-necked hornbill with his sharp sinister cry, the rare and elegant egret, the pink flamingo with his fragile legs, and the isolated golden oriole

Ceylon

whose raucous and impertinent call seems so at variance with his distinguished and colourful body.

From Mankulam the enterprising traveller can go east to Mullaittivu on the coast, a distance of thirty miles. For the jungle lover the road will be of absorbing interest, and he will probably wonder how so many creatures can live in a district which, except from November to January, is practically bereft of fresh water. Mullaittivu itself is of small interest, and the average visitor will gain little additional knowledge of the island from this journey.

Returning to the Mankulam-Jaffna road (the distance separating these towns is sixty-one miles), the jungle continues in equal density for the twenty-one miles to Parantan, when the forest gives way to scrub and sand until, after a further stretch of seven miles, the Elephant Pass is reached which connects the peninsula of Jaffna with the mainland. Here begins the typical vegetation of the peninsula: vast expanses of sand dotted with palmyra palms alternating with areas under constant cultivation. The name of Elephant Pass is said to be derived from the quantities of elephants which cross from the mainland in order to devour the ripe fruit of the palmyra. The pass itself borders a large lagoon in which excellent "Seer"

Pleasant Journeys

fishing can be enjoyed. On the edge of this placid water stands one of the prettiest rest-houses in Ceylon. It is an authentic relic of the seventeenth century, little changed since the time of the Dutch. The remaining thirty-three miles to Jaffna pass through palmyra plantations, with the continuous and drab company of the railway on the left, and, since the road is otherwise of little interest, there is time to consider the ubiquitous palmyra together with other less important products of this prosperous peninsula.

The palmyra is to the north of Ceylon what the coconut is to the southern and central provinces. It is a tree, like the coconut, which has so many uses that the sight of it must often bring tears to the eyes of the frugal Frenchman when he considers that it will not grow in similar profusion in France. The wood of the palmyra is very hard, and it makes strong furniture and durable roofs. From the sap "toddy" (the Ceylonese equivalent of beer) is made. The leaves are used for fans, fencing, mats, manure, baskets, and form a ready-made umbrella. The seeds are used in flour and curry, and even the husks make satisfactory fuel. The appearance of the palmyra varies in an astonishing manner. Sometimes above its towering rough trunk green and gold leaves rustle in the

Ceylon

breeze like the feathers on some fabulous headdress. Then again one isolated specimen, crowned with a short shaggy tuft, makes an ungainly if humorous blot in the landscape. After the palmyra tobacco is the most important industry in the peninsula, but being strong and coarse it appeals to few European palates. Owing to lack of sufficient water, there are few paddy-fields to be seen, "Kurukkan" and other forms of millet taking their place. The gourmet will notice with satisfaction the tidy little gardens on the roadside, in which many varieties of herbs and spices are grown for his curry.

At Pallai, twenty-two miles from Jaffna, the palms are replaced by a number of coconut estates, and having mentioned the uses of the palmyra it may be interesting briefly to consider those of the coconut. The root of this beautiful tree is used for medicines and firewood, the trunk for fencing and roofs, the ekel for garden brooms, and the leaves of the coconut make an excellent thatch. From the fruit itself Arrack (a potent white liqueur) and toddy are distilled, while the actual "milk," besides making a delicious cool drink, is used in *hoppers* and curries. From the husk coir ropes are woven, and mattresses are stuffed with the fibre, which is a far cooler substance than

Pleasant Journeys

wool. Indeed, the coconut, being more prolific in its multifarious uses than the palmyra, should invite even greater envy and curiosity on the part of the French.

The rest-house at Jaffna is in the middle of the town but, although its position is noisy, it is comfortable and spacious and the curries served by an amiable host are as good as anywhere in the island. The first thing the visitor will notice about this pleasant but amorphous town is the striking difference, both in physiognomy and costume, between the Jaffna Tamils and the other inhabitants of Ceylon. The men are coarser and more virile in appearance than the Singalese, and their industrious habits leave them little time for the loitering and gossip which are so prevalent in other parts of the island. Western clothes are rarely seen, and all the men wear the white *veti*, or cloth, and affect little colour in comparison with the Singalese. The women, however, who very properly rarely walk in the streets without carrying something on their heads, delight in the brightest colours, red and yellow being their favourites, and it should be noticed that, in contrast to the Singalese women who wear the *sari* finishing in a loose end over the right shoulder, the ladies of Jaffna carry their upper cloth straight round the body

Ceylon

under the arms, leaving the neck and shoulders uncovered.

Another peculiarity of these people is the cavernous houses in which they live. Windows in these edifices are unknown, and they consist of four high walls, a thatched roof and a back door. These strange and insalubrious habitations are often used as business premises as well; but the Tamil does not display his goods, being too apprehensive of his neighbour, and a prospective customer is compelled to put his head through a gap in the protecting fence and to call out for any commodity he may require. All these elaborate precautions against theft have induced some unwary writers on Ceylon to compare the Tamil to the Scot.

A short walk down Main Street, or in the near neighbourhood, where there are many houses of Dutch origin, will familiarize the visitor with the industrious and peace-loving inhabitants of the town, and after a really delicious rice and curry at the rest-house he will be, or anyhow should be, anxious to visit the famous Dutch fort, which is the principal reason for visiting Jaffna and is certainly one of the most impressive buildings in Ceylon. Originally constructed by the Portuguese in the sixteenth century, it was considerably enlarged after being captured by the Dutch in 1658.

Pleasant Journeys

It faces boldly across the sea, and the great expanse of dark grey ramparts, defended at the corners with robust *tourelles*, is reminiscent of a French twelfth-century château. Large tracts of water separate the inner and the outer walls, and the whole is dominated by a great red-roofed church, which rises from the inner ward with majestic solidity.

The spacious interior of the fort resembles, with obvious modifications, the peaceful close of an English cathedral, with low, unpretentious houses covered with different shades of bougainvillea. The big, cruciform church is of course always locked, but on the visitor's approach an eager youth will appear with an immense key and open the wooden entrance door, over which is inscribed the date of construction, 1706. The interior of the church, which is rather reminiscent of a derelict law court, is gaunt and oppressive, even for a conventicle erected for the rites of the Dutch Reformed Church, but there are many delightful objects deserving inspection. The most noteworthy is the screen of the low organ gallery, which is supported on the ugly bulbous legs of the period, with a grille on either side. In the centre projects an amusing coloured bas-relief depicting a bald King David playing the harp, while

Ceylon

a sheep and an ass, sheltering under a palm tree, form an interested audience. This is probably the work of a Tamil artist. The large simple font is noticeable for its good proportions, and the wooden pulpit, resembling some gargantuan goblet, is at least a singular work of art.

The visitor will also be interested in some fine brasses, memorials to Dutch officials of the fort, and he may wonder how production of this calibre came to be carried out in the island. The answer is that when the Dutchman of the seventeenth century set out for Ceylon he knew that there was little chance of his ever returning to Holland; therefore, together with his more transitory belongings such as wife and children, he also brought along his tomb. A flamboyant memorial on the wall to an Admiral Reder will also catch the visitor's eye, as well as some obituary tablets to various English officers and their wives, the last bearing the date of 1850. Shortly after, the fort becoming obsolete, the troops were withdrawn and this spacious church, which had been the conventicle in turn of both Dutch and English Protestants, fell into desuetude. The Christian Tamils, however, nearly all belong to the Catholic Church, and are naturally proud of their inspiring legend that the coloured monarch who visited the crib at Bethlehem was

Pleasant Journeys

none other than the contemporary King of Jaffna, Gaspar Peria-Perumal.

Before leaving the peninsula, the visitor with time at his disposal can spend a delightful week-end at Kankesanturai, eleven miles north of Jaffna, in an excellent and remote rest-house, situated on a strip of land jutting into the sea. Thence he can visit Point Pedro, the most easternly place on the peninsula, which is fifteen miles from Kankesanturai, along a fine coast road. At Point Pedro there is one of the most beautiful Hindu temples in Ceylon. Ten rows of little figures, the sacred bull predominating, rise on the façade and are crowned by an elegant, gilded pagoda. No doubt in a short time these delightful figures will be garishly repainted, as unfortunately is the general habit of the Hindus, and their pleasant charm thereby destroyed. The exteriors of Hindu temples are usually crude and barbaric in appearance and contrast unfavourably with the more sober façades of Buddhist shrines. Nevertheless, no aesthetic crimes committed by the Hindus can compare to those freely perpetrated with paint by the Buddhists on some of their most magnificent figures of the Gautama Buddha.

Our visit to the Jaffna peninsula is now concluded, but in order to continue the journey to

Ceylon

Mannar on the west coast it is necessary to return to Jaffna and thence to Vavuniya on the same road on which we came. A further sixteen miles south on this road brings the traveller to Madawachchiya, where the route to Mannar turns north-west to the coast.

A visit to Mannar is by no means essential, although it is more interesting than that to Mullaittivu, despite the ugly scenery from Madawachchiya to the sea. Sir James Tennent, writing angrily in the 'fifties of this neighbourhood (every visitor should read his *Ceylon*), describes it as "sterile and repulsive, covered by a stunted growth of umbrella trees and buffalo horns." Sir James may be a trifle severe, but these objects still remain the chief decoration of the landscape. The ubiquitous skulls are the result of a waterless district, where at the end of the dry season in September scores of buffalo, searching for a tank, slowly die from lack of water. The "umbrella" trees are in fact baobabs originally imported from Africa. They are indeed hideous, possessing a circumference of about thirty feet, which usually equals, and sometimes exceeds, the total height of the tree. They have an added curiosity in being practically leafless. For me these horns and baobabs had a singular and sinister resemblance: the

Pleasant Journeys

skulls long denuded of flesh and skin paralleled by these lifeless trees bereft of flower and foliage.

Mannar is on an island which is reached by a cumbersome chain ferry across a narrow and picturesque lagoon. It is protected seawards by a small Dutch fort, stretching down to the yellow sands, which are fringed by cactus and covered with pink shells. Mannar is famous for its pearl fishery and for the chanks which are found in profusion in the neighbouring Palk Bay. Chanks are large shells which, fashioned into personal ornaments, are placed on the dead at Hindu funerals. The Buddhists also value chanks and, after being perforated, they use them as trumpets in their temples. The connection of Mannar with pearls and chanks is two thousand five hundred years old, since, in the sixth century B.C., the first King of Ceylon, Vijaya, propitiated his father-in-law in India with a cargo of pearls and chanks worth two lacs of rupees.

On leaving Mannar there is no choice but to return on the same road to Madawachchiya; thence due south to Anuradhapura is a distance of fifteen miles. The country now becomes gradually less arid until the most important of the "Lost Cities" is reached. Anuradhapura is described in an earlier chapter, but if the traveller happens to follow the

Ceylon

five routes forming my "Pleasant Journeys," it should be either visited at this juncture or else on Journey "D," when the road will be taken from Colombo to Kekirawa, via Negombo, Chilaw, Puttalam, and Anuradhapura.

The route from Anuradhapura to Trincomalee, a distance of sixty-five miles, covers perhaps the finest jungle road in Ceylon, but I used it so often as to be prejudiced in its favour. Certainly it is not so remote as the east coast road or that, for example, from Hambantota to Wellawaya, but the traveller who loves good timber and the sights of the jungle will be amply rewarded on this route. Incidentally, the view of and from Mihintale, which is eight miles east of Anuradhapura and described in the chapter on that city, is one of the most beautiful in Ceylon. It is a distance of twenty-four miles from Mihintale to Horawapotana through solid jungle and virgin forest, although unfortunately increasing traffic is making the animals more wary of the road. At Horawapotana the traveller rejoins the road on which he set out for the Jaffna peninsula.

This is the end of our second "Pleasant Journey."

PLEASANT JOURNEYS

✡

C—*Trincomalee to Kantalai, Kekirawa, Dambulla, Nalanda, Matale, and Kandy. The three routes from Kandy to Colombo: (1) via Kurunegala and Negombo, one hundred miles; (2) via Ginigathena Gap and Avisawella, ninety-five miles; (3) via Kegalla and Veyangoda, seventy-two miles.*

The road from Trincomalee to Kantalai, a distance of twenty-six miles, differs little from that to Horawapotana except in so far as the timber appears older and more magnificent, the trees often touching overhead to form a green arcade. In my experience, this is a road much frequented by monkeys, and on it the keen photographer can have a busy time attempting to take pictures of these fascinating but wary animals. As Kantalai possesses, in my opinion, the most beautiful tank in Ceylon, I hope I may be able to persuade the traveller to linger there by a brief description of this delightful locality.

I arrived at this tank, which was built by King Mahasena in the fourth century B.C., in time to

Ceylon

enjoy the sunset, as every visitor should attempt to do. I approached from the south on a straight road running on the high bund, with impenetrable jungle on the right, and on the left some fifty yards of gently sloping parkland stretching to the edge of the tank. Here at night "sportsmen" lie in wait for the bear as he comes to refresh himself at its dark waters. The sun sets behind the village of Kantalai, and as I drove along the bund the tank was shining like golden glass, in which the homing flocks of cormorant and crane were mirrored like little flecks of ebony and snow.

I rose at five-thirty to enjoy the dawn, and in the first light of the hidden sun a sable peninsula, jutting from the north-east bank, broke the grey texture of the lake as a blade of darkened steel. Slowly the waters turned to a vivid yellow, revealing an army of cormorants drawn up in lines, as if in array of battle after the night's rest. As the sun awakened them, they rose like a black cloud from the edge of the now pale green peninsula and dispersed for the morning meal. Their raucous cries aroused from the far side of the tank flocks of flamingoes, pelicans and cranes, so that the rising sun became overcast with a moving panorama of screeching and colourful birds.

Pleasant Journeys

It was on this tank that I first made the acquaintance of the so-called "Snake-bird," one of the most attractive and astonishing of Ceylonese waterfowl. It derives its name from the curious habit of swimming with the body submerged, so that, its long neck alone being visible, it appears like a snake gliding upright on the water. A large flock of these birds in the water presents a most uncanny spectacle, and it is quite a surprise to realize they have bodies when, leaving the water, they stand motionless on the rocks, with wide brown wings extended in the sun.

The rest-house itself makes a delightful background from which the visitor can view the ever-changing scene at Kantalai. It stands high above the tank on massive rocks, a short distance from an insignificant village. The most striking feature of the interior is a large wire cage, in a thin mesh, provided with a door and a pantry trap. This erection serves as a welcome escape from the swarms of mosquitoes and ground insects which devour the visitor during the rains from September to November. Once inside this human larder, refreshments are only served through the trap, and it is highly inadvisable to venture outside unless provided with top-boots, thick gloves, and a veil. Those who might find this mode of living painful

Ceylon

rather than humorous are strongly advised to avoid Kantalai during the rainy season.

It is twenty-seven miles through thick jungle to Habarane, whence Polonnaruwa (described in the chapter on the "Lost Cities") should be visited, taking a road to the left after passing through Habarane. Fourteen miles along this twisting jungle route lies the beautiful tank of Minneriya built, like that at Kantalai, by King Mahasena. It is pleasant to refresh oneself on the banks of this vast reservoir, with its circumference of over thirty miles. It may also be an appropriate moment to take out one's "Tennent" and to read that Minneriya evoked in the imagination of Sir James "visions of Killarney, warmed and illumined by an Eastern sun." A further ten miles from Minneriya will bring the traveller to Polonnaruwa. This "lost city" is fully described in a previous chapter, but it should be mentioned here that the rest-house is excellent and finely situated on the shore of the great Topawewa tank, which was constructed by King Upatissa during the fourth century A.D. Although more famous than Kantalai, Topawewa does not, in my opinion, approach that tank in beauty. Topawewa seems like a boundless ocean across which the eye cannot carry, while Kantalai gives the soothing impression of a fair domestic reservoir.

Pleasant Journeys

After visiting Polonnaruwa, the traveller must take the same road back to Habarane whence, turning left on the main Kandy route, he will find, after six miles, a small road to the left leading to Sigiriya. As this road leads only to the "Lion Rock" (which has had a chapter to itself) the beauty of the jungle is now increased by the absence of traffic, and the consequent greater profusion of animal life. This road is famous for the hatch of white butterflies which frequents it just before the rains. I remember once my car being enveloped in such a dense cloud of these lovely insects that it was necessary to proceed at no more than ten miles an hour. Nevertheless, countless numbers were killed on the radiator, and they poured through the open windows like wind-driven flakes of snow. The butterflies were all heading in the same direction as the car, and I was fortunate enough to discover the object of their flight in the bed of a small stream in a clearing in the jungle. Here they were massed in thousands round shallow pools, the green of their inner wings likening them to fresh shoots of paddy as they sat motionless by the water.

Another delightful distinction of this road is the continuous array of golden anthills on either side. Ants in Ceylon appear to have a keen sense of

Ceylon

decoration, judging by the variety and elaboration of the homes they build. Those interested in the history of architecture will notice amongst these gay erections rough facsimiles of Norman castles, Jacobean halls and Rococo pavilions, although the most fashionable style appears to be Catalan in flavour, and many of the anthills are reminiscent of the Church of the "Sagrada Familia" in Barcelona.

As Sigiriya has been described in a previous chapter, it is here only necessary to remark on the remoteness and excellence of the rest-house which is situated half a mile from the "Lion Rock," and of which it enjoys a most beautiful view. The recollection of one dinner I enjoyed there lingers in my memory. It was served by the distinguished Singalese rest-house keeper with grey hair and the manners of a French *maître d'hôtel*. The meal began with hare soup, which was followed by jungle fowl, wild pig and snipe, since in this rest-house it is unnecessary to rely for sustenance on rice and curry. I was sitting on the verandah digesting this delicious meal, when a pack of jackals passed close to the compound, uttering their weird and ruthless cries. Fortunately for my self-composure I could not see them, since visibility that night was bad owing to the proximity of the rains. Indeed, all I could make out from

Pleasant Journeys

the verandah was a hoary banyan-tree a few yards off, which appeared strangely like an elephant with its head buried in the sand. Around the gnarled roots rose a pile of buffalo skulls, and above this sinister mass sat a large owl, resembling a bearded savant, watching me with unblinking and startled eyes. The whole scene was in singular contrast with the homely atmosphere of this rest-house, where no traveller should fail to stay.

Leaving Sigiriya and returning to Habarane, the road north to Kekirawa must be taken, a distance of twelve miles through the jungle. I have such a lively and happy recollection of Kekirawa that I hope the visitor will not be disappointed with it since, after Arugam Bay and Kalkuda, I know of no more delightful neighbourhood in the island. Kekirawa has an additional advantage in being situated almost in the centre of Ceylon, and for the traveller who prefers an occasional fixed headquarters to packing his bag every morning for a different rest-house, Kekirawa is an ideal locality. From this remote and unspoilt village the most important architectural and historical monuments of the island can be visited within a radius of twenty-five miles. These include Anuradhapura, Polonnaruwa, Sigiriya, Dambulla, Yapahuwa, and Kalawewa.

Ceylon

For the traveller to make Kekirawa his headquarters presupposes the existence of a good rest-house, and I may be influenced by an abiding recollection of courtesy, comfort, and palatable curry when I say that in the rest-house keeper at Kekirawa the visitor will find no better host in Ceylon. He was tall and grave with a large grey *konde*, or bun, at the back of his head, placed in the same position as Queen Victoria wore hers on coming to the throne. While the rest-house keeper at Sigiriya resembled, as I suggested, a distinguished *maître d'hôtel*, the host at Kekirawa reminded me of pictures of Leo XIII. Apart from his own active and vigilant service, the rest-house was served by his two sons, aged ten and eleven, who were the acme of liveliness and efficiency. Their mother cooked as well as any, but of course was never visible, and apart from these there were no other servants in the house. I shall long cherish the memory of that courteous and delightful family. As for the rest-house itself, it is most commodious and picturesque, being happily situated amidst banyans and tulip trees. The west side of the compound faces the jungle, while the east touches the village, although the latter does not disturb its genial solitude.

One of the most beautiful roads in Ceylon leads

29. An Anthill in the Jungle (See page 261)

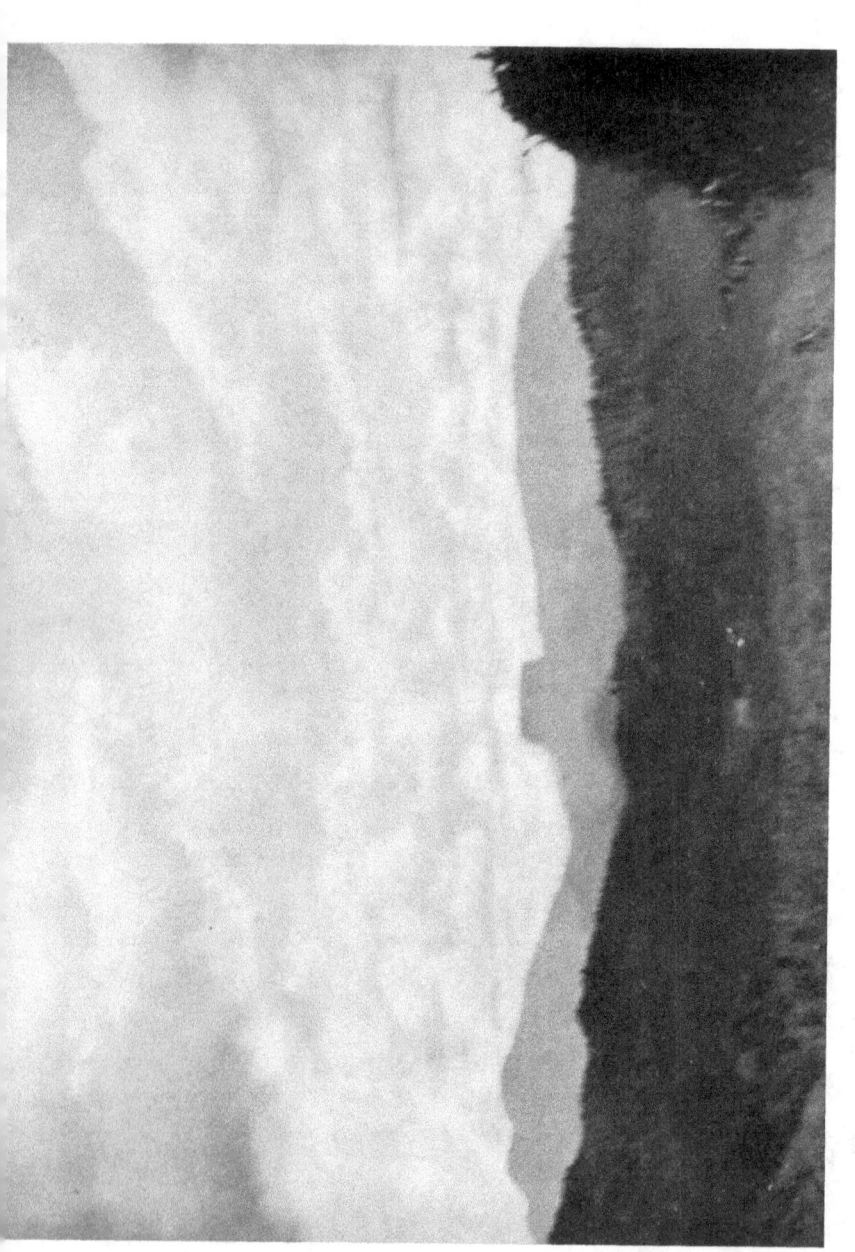

30. The "Bible" Rock (See page 278)

Pleasant Journeys

from Kekirawa to Talawa, a distance of twenty-three miles, north-west of the former village. This road, so rarely explored by the visitor, is lined on either side with tanks of every size and configuration, since this country was once on the outskirts of Anuradhapura and the tanks irrigated the paddy-fields on which existed that city's population of five million souls. Sometimes a tank will lie directly on the roadside, perhaps covered with the red lotus and the haunt of snipe and crane. The existence of other tanks will be indicated by the presence of a high bund, which on being scaled may reveal a large expanse of glittering water or else a few pools in an otherwise dry reservoir. In the latter, perhaps, a semi-nude fisherman may be catching fish in his basket-trap, or again a somnolent buffalo may raise an unfriendly head from his cushion of mud.

Ten miles along this enchanting road from Kekirawa there is a left-hand turn to Kalawewa tank, from which, after a gruelling walk of two miles through the jungle, the traveller may reach the Aukana Vehera, described in an earlier chapter. Now, however, I would presume that the visitor, having improved his mind at this magnificent shrine, is prepared to continue on the road to Talawa, thirteen miles away. Possibly, like myself,

Ceylon

he will carry a gun on this expedition, and if so he should enjoy some excellent snipe-shooting. The choice of tank, however, is not easy. The great tank of Talawa is normally too full of ladies washing to make shooting practicable, apart from the deterrent factor that Singalese women, being more modest than their European sisters, strongly resent the approach of the male when they are bathing. But the Kanthriyagama tank, rather less than half-way on the road to Talawa, is usually devoid of human beings, although by no means free of buffalo, and is an ideal locality for shooting. There are a few cottages in the vicinity from which a "retriever," in the shape of a small brown boy, can easily be obtained. This assistance is essential, as no normal-sized European could walk in the mud at the edge of the tank without sinking, while crocodiles, which abound in its waters, are uninterested in the edible attractions of a native leg. This tank is covered with the lotus, and many besides myself may enjoy the rare experience of killing snipe amongst the red blooms of this exotic flower. Others, however, may more properly consider that such pleasures are to be abhorred.

The traveller must now perforce leave behind the charms of Kekirawa and Talawa and take the road south from Kekirawa to Kandy. The **main**

Pleasant Journeys

road from Trincomalee is joined, after a run of twelve miles, at Dambulla. Except for the famous rock temple already described, Dambulla is a drab little town and, on leaving it, the scenery gradually changes, the jungle receding into the distance to be replaced by stretches of uninteresting scrub, alternating with large tea, coconut and rubber plantations. Nalanda is fourteen miles from Dambulla, and the village is overshadowed by two giant twin peaks of the same name. The traveller should like Nalanda, with its wealth of variegated timber, and he will find it convenient to stay there in a pleasantly situated rest-house, in order to visit the ruins of the beautiful Gedi-Gé, to which reference has been made. This temple, which is a mile from the rest-house, is approached by a track running down one of the most breathless little valleys to be found in Ceylon.

It is fifteen miles from Nalanda to Matale through highly cultivated country, and the road is shaded by avenues of palms or coconuts all the way. Plantains and breadfruit are also much in evidence, while the pepper-plant will be noticed growing up many of the trees. The country is no longer wild and remote, and many like myself may long to return to the jungle when driving through this populous and sophisticated countryside. Two miles

Ceylon

before reaching Matale the traveller passes the romantic Temple of Aluvihare, already described, which he is certain to visit. Matale is a busy town with a gay bazaar, and here lovers of the "Arts and Crafts" can buy jolly little lacquer boxes and gaudy but useless fans. Shortly after leaving Matale on the sixteen-mile stretch to Kandy, the road curves brusquely through the Balakaduwa pass, where magnificent views can be enjoyed towards the south and Adam's Peak.

Kandy, which in Singalese is called "Maha-Nuwara," or the "Great City," is a delightful as well as an historic town with a certain choice of comfortable accommodation, the Queen's being one of the best hotels in the East. The most important monument is the Temple of the Tooth, which, together with its two adjacent shrines, has already been described. After these the most interesting building is the Old Palace, almost adjoining the temple. As it is now the residence of the Government Agent, permission must be obtained to visit the interior.

The two existing buildings of the Old Palace are all that remain of the residence of the kings of Kandy, and they date from the eighteenth century. These are the edifice inhabited by the Agent, which once housed the royal ladies, and the Audi-

Pleasant Journeys

ence Hall, now used as the Supreme Court. The roof of the latter is supported by carved pillars in the florid style which is typical of the later Kandyan architecture. In this hall, built by King Rajadi Raja Sinha in 1784, "the monarch," according to Mrs. Heber, the wife of the Anglican bishop, "used to show himself in state to his people with a wife on either hand." Mrs. Heber's surprise at this ceremonial must have been enhanced by the spectacle of the courtiers entering and leaving the presence on all fours.

There is a delightful reception room in the Old Palace decorated in bas-relief, with panels of dancing-women holding large fans over their heads and heraldic animals, amongst which predominate the sacred goose and the Singalese lion. Rounded arches give access to this room, and the walls are painted pale blue with the bas-reliefs in white. For some years past the authorities have been preparing a scheme for turning the Old Palace into a museum, with the principal object of accommodating the Kandyan regalia now at Colombo. Behind the Temple of the Tooth there is a rather inadequate museum containing relics of the kings, some crude agricultural implements and a large variety of modern Kandyan "crafts," which can be bought by the acquisitive visitor.

Ceylon

For many, however, the principal charm of Kandy will lie in its beautiful position and in the delightful walks and drives which can be taken in the neighbourhood. The main part of the town is situated round an oval lake, surrounded by high hills timbered with palms and flowering trees. Two sides of the lake are edged with a bund which is surmounted by a parapet, the design being copied from the balustrade on the Temple of the Tooth. The lake was built by the last King of Kandy, Sri Wikrama Raja Sinha, as a defence against attempted assassination. In the middle of the waters there is a small island ornamented with a crumbling arch, where the King's unsatisfactory wives passed in duress their declining years.

There are four principal walks or drives in the neighbourhood of Kandy: the Upper Lake Road and one walk and two drives named after the beneficent wives of three former Governors: the Ladies Horton, Longden and Blake. The Upper Lake Road, which entails an arduous climb, lies across the bridge opposite Queen's Hotel and leads to Wace Park. Here a beautiful view of Kandy can be obtained. Lady Horton's walk begins by the gates of the King's Pavilion, the Governor's residence, which was built over a hundred years ago by Sir Edward Barnes, who was also responsible

Pleasant Journeys

for Mount Lavinia. This walk leads through woodland, with occasional glimpses of the lake below. Lady Longden's drive begins on the left-hand side of the lake by the tennis-courts. Emerging into Malabar Street, it continues up Lady McCarthy's drive, which leads to Lady Gordon's road. The latter comes out eventually into Trincomalee Street, after passing above the beautiful Dumbara Valley. The entrance to Lady Blake's drive is up Halloluwa Road, on the right-hand side of the Peradeniya Road coming from Kandy. It leads away from the lake through woods and paddy-fields and descends to the broad waters of the Mahaweliganga. The drive ends on the Peradeniya Road. Space unfortunately prevents a fuller description of these delightful walks and drives, but the visitor when enjoying their charm and variety should reflect on the foresight of those important Victorian ladies who, in their polite anxiety to take "carriage exercise," were responsible for their construction.

There are four other objects of interest in the neighbourhood of Kandy: the Royal Botanic Gardens, the Lankatilaka and the Gadaladeniya temples, and the village of Udugalpitiya. These gardens, which are one of Ceylon's proudest possessions, lie on the Peradeniya Road a short distance

Ceylon

outside Kandy. They were originally laid out in 1821 and cover an area of one hundred and forty-three acres, being one thousand five hundred and fifty feet above sea-level and enjoying a mean annual temperature of seventy degrees Fahrenheit. The following brief notes on these fascinating gardens may be of help to the visitor, who should bear in mind that March and April are the best months for flowers, trees and flowering shrubs, although at most times of the year there is colour and always interest in the Royal Botanic Gardens.

(1) The entrance gates are hung with a creeper called "Bignonia unguis." In March it trails garlands of yellow blossom.

(2) From the gate, the main drive is bordered in March with white lilies, and later there are red hibiscus, golden tabebuia and purple jacaranda.

(3) The first turning on the right leads to the flower garden, with a pond of aquatic plants surrounded by Assam rubber trees. Along the stream grow the fly-catching pitcher plants and the exotic sealing-wax palm with its pillar-box red stem.

(4) Nearby the large conservatories grow varieties of orchids, antirrhinum, acalypha and Eucharist lilies. These houses are backed by beds of cannas, salvias and poinsettias, encircled by arches of the sinister aristolochia, a fly-catcher, and red

Pleasant Journeys

ipomoea, clerodendron, and pink antigonon. These arches lead to the Bat Drive, where quantities of flying foxes can be seen hanging head downwards from the banyan trees.

(5) Returning to the carriage drive and passing the rather uninteresting fruit trees, the road leads to the River Drive along the Mahaweliganga where, amidst a rich variety, the cannon-ball tree can be seen, with its pink flowers and clumsy seed-pods, and a group of giant bamboos which, in March, are credited with a growth of two feet a night.

(6) The first turning on the left from the River Drive leads to an avenue of palmyras overshadowing banks of pink cassias, which in April and May bear a flower like a large hawthorn.

(7) Further along the river lies the Arboretum, through which many twisting paths invite the visitor to enjoy a walk.

(8) After passing, on the right, the road to the ferry, the next turning leads to the Grand Circle of royal palms, but if the visitor continues on the River Drive the road to the right after the ferry road will bring him to perhaps the most attractive feature of the gardens, the Talipot Avenue. These graceful trees have a life of about seventy years and, on flowering, die. Their leaf, besides pro-

Ceylon

tecting the *bhikkhu* against sun and rain, were in earlier years also used by laymen, since Robert Knox sententiously refers to the talipot as "a marvellous mercy which Almighty God hath bestowed upon this poor and naked people."

(9) Before leaving the gardens the visitor should inspect the Museum near the Bat Drive. Beside an exhibition of Ceylonese woods, there is an interesting collection of the different insects which devour vegetation. These include the common but fascinating "praying-mantis," an insect which when motionless appears to be engaged in its devotions.

Amongst the three remaining objects of interest in the vicinity are the temples of Gadaladeniya and Lankatilaka. The former is situated on the Peradeniya Road and, having crossed the bridge, a right turn must be made in the direction of Kadugannawa. After nine miles the road to Daulagalla must be taken, and just before reaching this village the traveller will arrive at the base of the high rock on which Gadaladeniya stands. The architecture of this temple, built in 1347, is graceful and regular, and a contemporary rock inscription on the outside wall will interest the archaeologist. The main features of the interior are the lacquered doors which protect the conventional statue of Buddha. Although repainted, these are very fine

Pleasant Journeys

and date from the fourteenth century. From the court of Gadaladeniya the Lankatilaka temple can be seen on the summit of an adjacent hill. To reach it, however, it is necessary to walk two miles along a footpath from Gadaladeniya, although it can also be approached from the road to Gampola, turning off by the Nanu-oya to Daulagalla. From this village a breathless walk of three miles brings the visitor to Lankatilaka. The temple, the name of which means "Crown of Ceylon," was also built in the fourteenth century and it is beautifully situated on the slope of a dark mountain. It is approached by a massive flight of steps, but the interior is undistinguished. Its exterior, however, is impressive, and it has been compared not without reason to a typical church in Norway.

The last excursion which I had suggested earlier in this section was that to Udugalpitiya, a village which lies between Gadaladeniya and Kadugannawa. Here lives the lowest caste in Ceylon, known as "Rodiya," which translated means "dung." The inhabitants received this unhappy appellation over a thousand years ago, when they attempted to feed the king of the period on human flesh. The outraged monarch then commanded that they and their descendants should be for ever treated as unclean outcasts. In consequence the severest

Ceylon

punishment that could be given to a Singalese lady of royal rank was to banish her to Udugalpitiya, where she was incorporated in the race by a "Rodiya" taking a betel leaf from his mouth and placing it in hers; "after which," remarks Sir James Tennent, "till death, her degradation was indelible." Although under British rule, the "Rodiyas" enjoy the same privileges as their fellow countrymen, even to-day, if a "Rodiya's" shadow darkens the rice-bowl of a devout Buddhist he will throw his food away. The village of Udugalpitiya is picturesque and the inhabitants very handsome, perhaps owing to the distant strain of royal blood in their veins. Unfortunately, however, for the good name of "Rodiyan" ladies they still indulge in dancing and legerdemain, two female occupations which are held in abhorrence by the more earnest Singalese. As a result of this attitude the visitor will never see women dancing in Ceylon, except in Udugalpitiya and in certain doubtful quarters, and at first he will be surprised to learn that the highly painted and feminine figures which may occasionally entertain him on the verandah of a rest-house are all boys.

The traveller has the choice of three alternative routes from Kandy to Colombo: (1) via Kurunegala and Negombo, one hundred miles; (2) via

Pleasant Journeys

Ginigathena Gap and Avisawella, ninety-five miles; (3) via Kegalla and Veyangoda, seventy-two miles. On the first route it is twenty-six miles to Kurunegala through the steep Galagedava pass and large plantations of rubber, coconut and tea. Although pleasantly situated by a large tank, Kurunegala is thought by many to be the hottest town in Ceylon. It is surrounded by huge rocks, the sinister Elephant Rock predominating. These appear to accumulate intense heat during the day, which later is exuded into the night air. The added incidence that Kurunegala harbours swarms of malarial mosquitoes during the rains also detracts from its popularity amongst European visitors. The fifty-one miles from Kurunegala to Negombo are passed along an undulating and shadeless road, but after Giriulla paddy-fields alternate with coconut plantations until ten miles from Negombo, when only coconuts meet the eye. Negombo itself, and the delightful road thence to Colombo, are described in the next section of "Pleasant Journeys."

The second route from Kandy to Colombo, via the Ginigathena Gap and Avisawella, passes at first along the Peradeniya Road to Gampola, a distance of twelve miles, where the steep descent of the Gap begins. The views at this point are magnificent although, unlike the jungle, they can be

Ceylon

paralleled by many in Europe. About eleven miles from Yatiyantota the low country begins, and continues through undistinguished scenery to Avisawella. After passing this town the road runs by the Kelani River all the way to Colombo, a distance of thirty miles. There is a delightful rest-house at Hanwella on the edge of the river, inviting the traveller to linger there. Hanwella has also historical associations, since here the last King of Kandy was finally defeated by the British in 1815. Kaduwela, ten miles from Colombo, also possesses a rest-house on the Kelani.

The third route from Kandy to Colombo, via Kegalla and Veyangoda, was opened in 1822. It is considerably the shortest, and therefore more often used by the traveller. For the same reason it is more crowded with traffic and less pleasant to use than the other two routes I have mentioned. After passing the Botanical Gardens on the Kegalla road, the route slowly descends through the Kadugannawa pass to the Mahaweliganga, which is Ceylon's most important river, flowing into the sea at Trincomalee. Before reaching Kegalla, twenty-three miles from Kandy, the well-situated rest-house at Mawanella is passed, while on the left a magnificent view can be enjoyed of the "Bible Rock," perhaps the most fascinating geological

Pleasant Journeys

formation in Ceylon. This rock, which should be seen at sunset, certainly bears a remarkable resemblance to a book, although none in particular to a Bible.

Before reaching Kegalla, stands another rock of massive proportions, named after a famous brigand of the 'fifties called Sardiel, who lived in the vicinity. It is related how after his capture by the English and sentence to death, a clergyman importuned the brigand for several days to accept the tenets of the Anglican Church. Sardiel, however, preferred to die as he had lived, a devout Buddhist. After leaving Kegalla, a straggling town with the ruins of an old fort, the road leads through Ambepussa, which possesses a rest-house, to Veyangoda, a distance of twenty-four miles. Here is the large estate of Sir Solomon Bandaranaike, with an enclosure by the road containing some animals indigenous to Ceylon. The country through which the traveller is now passing is rich in paddy-fields and, there being a lack of other interests, except for coconuts already discussed, the moment seems appropriate to mention paddy.

The cultivation of paddy inevitably surprises the traveller at first since, in the same neighbourhood and at similar seasons, fields can be seen either inundated or in fallow, or again growing masses of

Ceylon

bright vegetation. The reason for these anomalies is that there are two crops annually, one harvested from January to March and called the "Maha," and a less fertile one called the "Yala" from August to October, while naturally certain expanses of soil must be allowed rest from cultivation under fallow. After the rains, ploughing begins with a single wooden instrument pulled by a buffalo, while in more remote parts of the country buffaloes are let loose in the fields to do what they can with their hooves. Then, after consulting the local astrologer, the village cultivator casts the seed on to the wet soil, which is afterwards inundated through adjacent channels of water connected with a tank. When the paddy begins to ripen the water is drawn off, and the fields are nearly dry by harvest-time. It is interesting to remember that the rice is grown entirely for Ceylonese consumption, but that nevertheless it is necessary to import large quantities from India. The emerald-green paddy-fields are beautiful to the eye, especially when dotted with white cranes.

The road from Veyangoda to the outskirts of Colombo, a distance of some twenty miles, varies little, although the traveller will pass through one very unusual village, the name of which is better unmentioned. The road through it is lined with

Pleasant Journeys

little stalls, behind which stand Singalese women selling cadjous. These nuts are indeed excellent, but the visitor may wonder why the vendors offer to their customers such smiles of encouragement. The reason given was that at night the stalls are illuminated with flares and that clients, other than those interested in cadjou nuts, are catered for. Such a spectacle is indeed rare in Ceylon, since Singalese women in general are an example to their sex.

I would like to relate one further personal experience on the road from Veyangoda to Colombo. This road is not only crowded with traffic, but also, through the villages, with fowls and pariahs. One of the former, a large white cock, was nearly run over by my car and, in rising to escape the front wheels, the bird was blown through the open windscreen on to my bare knees. The pain from its claws was considerable, and therefore, regarding his action as unfriendly, I seized the fowl and flung him through the open window on my left. My driver, however, did not approve of my violence, and with true Buddhist magnanimity quite seriously remarked that I was wrong in expelling the white cock from the car, since the bird was entitled to ask for a lift.

This is the end of our third "Pleasant Journey."

PLEASANT JOURNEYS

☼

D—*Colombo to Negombo, Chilaw, Kalpitiya, Puttalam, Anuradhapura, and Kekirawa*

In this "Pleasant Journey" I am assuming that the traveller shares my appreciation of Kekirawa as a tourist centre, and I am consequently taking him back there from Colombo on a new route, so that if it suits him he can enjoy Anuradhapura from Kekirawa, since it is far more convenient for this purpose than Trincomalee.

The road from Colombo to Negombo, a distance of twenty-three miles, lies mostly by the sea. There is a rest-house at Ja-ela, eleven miles along this rather crowded road, which passes through pretty coconut and cinnamon country. Cinnamon are not unlike tea bushes, and would grow to the height of an average tree unless they were vigorously pruned. The bark from the shoots is peeled off and dried to form the most popular and best-known spice of the East. Many other interesting trees can be studied along this route, including plantains, breadfruit, which when cooked tastes

Pleasant Journeys

like a turnip, dark green papaws with the delicious flavour of their rich orange flesh, and the pale green mango, in my opinion the most exquisite fruit in Ceylon.

Negombo, perhaps, is the most attractive of the smaller towns in the island. It is delightfully situated along a broad stretch of yellow strand, and the visitor will linger with pleasure in the narrow and shady streets of this peaceful and prosperous town. The fort, standing some distance from the sea, is small in comparison with those at Jaffna and Batticaloa, but it has a most compact and picturesque exterior. It was built by the Portuguese in the sixteenth century, and finally fell to the Dutch in 1644. Negombo also possesses a large and comfortable rest-house near the shore. Its tranquillity is only disturbed by a multitude of impudent crows. The bathing, which looks so inviting, is far from safe, except for the strongest swimmer, owing to a strong backwash and a steep decline of shifting sand.

Fishing is the principal industry of Negombo, and in the early morning the almost naked fishermen can be seen, either embarking in their orange-sailed "Catamarans" or pulling in their long brown nets on the shore. Shell fish abound, also sardines, whiting and the "seer," a fish with white

Ceylon

flesh and similar to the salmon in flavour. The fisher caste are nearly all Catholics, inheriting that faith from the Portuguese and preserving it during the long persecution by the Dutch. Negombo to-day is probably the most Catholic town in Ceylon, and I only hope that the traveller will visit it on some important feast-day, when he may enjoy a similar experience as the one I propose to relate.

Shortly before sunset I was walking on the sands when, in the distance against a background of giant coconuts, I saw a bright streak of colour winding along the shore. As it drew nearer I could distinguish a vast multitude of Singalese, who were chanting in unison around two raised platforms in their midst. The women, all hatless, were resplendent in their green, scarlet, and purple *saris*, while the men, with a dying eye for colour, were mostly dressed in singlet and trousers. The platforms, as they approached, proved to sustain two small statues of the Madonna and St. Sebastian, out of all proportion to the large green and gold *baldacchini* above them. But I recollected that a Singalese priest had told me that in order to avoid an exaggerated devotion to the Blessed Virgin and the saints, statues in Ceylon were always executed in a simple and unemotional manner.

Pleasant Journeys

I followed this devout crowd, which was entirely composed of laity, to the market square, where a halt was made and the rosary chanted in Singalese and with great piety, while all the people, including a policeman in my vicinity, participated in the devotion on their knees. Meanwhile near the market itself a large drum was being stationed with charcoal beneath it, in order to obtain the right degree of elasticity. Then ten or twelve women ceremoniously assumed sitting postures round the drum, as if they were going to enjoy a meal on its taut vellum surface. But instead they began to tap it with ever-increasing vigour as an accompaniment to their strangely mournful singing. I was told by an onlooker that the words of these songs were by no means all of a religious nature, many being of a mundane and even comic character.

Leaving Negombo with, I hope, profound regret the traveller will now take the road north to Chilaw, a distance of twenty-six miles, through some of the best coconut country in Ceylon. Chilaw with the remains of a Dutch fort is of slight interest, although there is a comfortable rest-house on the shore. Bathing here is exceptionally dangerous, but behind the rest-house lies a salt-water lagoon where the adventurous can

Ceylon

swim in the gay company of the inhabitants and a few innocuous animals. Before leaving Chilaw a visit should be made to the Hindu temple at Munesseram, a few miles along the Maho road. It is the best-preserved and most imposing of its type in the island. Returning to Chilaw the road runs north to Puttalam, a distance of thirty-three miles. After passing Battulu-oya, thirteen miles from Chilaw, the magnificent tank of Mundel is reached. This break in the endless stretch of coconut plantations is most welcome, although unfortunately there is no rest-house in the immediate vicinity.

Five miles before Puttalam the immense Etalai tank comes into view, and the traveller who wishes to visit the delightful fort at Kalpitiya should take the road to the left which fringes the western side of this beautiful stretch of water. Along its edge coconuts can be admired in their full splendour; their higher foliage swaying in the breeze like green ostrich feathers, their lower leaves matured to a burnished gold. There is twenty miles of deserted road to Kalpitiya, with the waters of the Etalai tank glittering through the coconuts on the right, while in the distance on the left lies the scrub on the seashore.

Kalpitiya is so rarely visited by tourists that

Pleasant Journeys

only an exiguous meal can be obtained at the rest-house unless notice has been previously given, but the fort is certainly one of the oldest and most picturesque in Ceylon. It faces due north towards Dutch Point Bay, and was erected by the Portuguese in the sixteenth century. Later it was rebuilt by the Dutch, and the date 1676 is conveniently inscribed over the entrance. The buildings in the interior appear to belong to the same period, but these were destroyed by fire more than a hundred years ago, and this once important stronghold is now a scene of eerie desolation. The dour exterior is surrounded by great lolling coconuts, and the small *tourelles* at every angle radiate an atmosphere of medieval defiance through the dark green shade. Kalpitiya is remote and beautiful, and well worthy of a visit from the discerning traveller.

The return must be made by the same route, and on reaching the main Chilaw-Puttalam road a sharp left turn leads to the latter town, after a short and pleasant drive on the eastern side of the Etalai tank. Puttalam is a large rambling town chiefly inhabited by Moors. The pearl fishery was established here over two thousand years ago, and it is still a source of considerable revenue. At Puttalam there is an excellent rest-house, while in the neighbourhood, at Madhu, the Catholics

Ceylon

possess the best-known church in Ceylon. Here a Passion play is annually performed, and owing to a much-revered statue of the Blessed Virgin it is a focus of pilgrimage, not only for Catholics, but also for throngs of Hindus and Buddhists, who on the Feast of the Assumption (August 15th) bring their sick to Madhu. This church might be called either a Ceylonese Lourdes or a Catholic Adam's Peak.

The distance from Puttalam to Anuradhapura is forty-seven miles along a road which, after crossing the Kala-oya, plunges once more into the jungle. To many it will be a relief when the endless coconut plantations, with their prosperous and sophisticated air, give way to the beasts and birds of the virgin forests. There are two roads from Anuradhapura to Kekirawa, both through the jungle. The shortest, via Tirappane, is twenty-five miles, but the traveller who at this point is anxious to visit Yapahuwa (already described) should take the road to Galgammuwa, thirty miles distant from Anuradhapura. On the way he will again pass Talawa, and a further ten miles will bring him to Galgammuwa. Here there is a charming rest-house situated on a small tank, surrounded on one side by a low bund, and on the others by forests and high irregular rocks. The Galgammuwa tank, three

31. Hindu Temple, Munesseram (See page 286)

32. Buffaloes bathing near Puttalam (See page 287)

Pleasant Journeys

miles away, is large and magnificent, the bund on the near side being over a hundred feet high. Massive rocks abound, while in the middle distance stretch large expanses of jungle and coconut country backed by dark mountains. It is seventeen miles along a primitive road from Galgammuwa, south-east to Yapahuwa, which is unprovided with a rest-house (1938). Thence it is a journey of twenty-five miles north-east to Kekirawa.

This track of country within the triangle formed by Anuradhapura, Galgammuwa, and Kekirawa— some of which was described in the previous "Pleasant Journey"—is, in my opinion, as fascinating as any in Ceylon. Here the traveller is never wearied by endless acres of the beautiful yet monotonous coconut, nor can he experience the sinister interminability of impenetrable jungle. In this country jungle, forest and cultivation share the landscape under a mutual if irregular agreement, and their spheres of domination are broken by great rocks, broad rivers and fair reservoirs. Talawa, Galgammuwa, Yapahuwa, Kekirawa and Talawewa, in themselves such beautiful names, bring back my most happy memories of Ceylon.

This is the end of our fourth "Pleasant Journey."

PLEASANT JOURNEYS

☼

E—*Kandy to Nuwara Eliya by two routes: (1) via Gampola and Ramboda Pass; (2) via Gampola, Nawalapitiya, Hatton, Maskeliya (Adam's Peak), and Talawakele. From Nuwara Eliya to Welimada, Badulla, Bandarawela, Haputale, Haldumulla, Balangoda, Ratnapura, Avisawella, and Colombo*

We now embark on the last of our "Pleasant Journeys" through what is known as "up-country." This expression is used of that part of Ceylon which is fifteen hundred feet above sea-level, the actual height of Kandy above the sea. This quarter of the island is a paradise for Europeans who live in Ceylon. The climate is mild compared to the low-country, the scenery is magnificent, and here golf, trout-fishing and even polo can be freely enjoyed. Many, including myself, who visited Ceylon neither with the objects of fishing nor of playing ball games may, however, prefer those parts of the island indigenous to the East to the lavish mountain scenery which can be paralleled, if not surpassed, in Europe. Nevertheless, in order to see the rubber and tea manufactories, which are

Pleasant Journeys

of great interest, it is necessary to visit this part of Ceylon.

There are two roads from Kandy to Nuwara Eliya, the first via Gampola and the Ramboda Pass, and the second via Gampola, Nawalapitiya, Hatton and Maskeliya. The former, which is the more direct, is a distance of forty-seven miles, and as far as Gampola, with its comfortable rest-house, leads through scrubby and uninteresting country. At Gampola the left-hand road must be taken, and after passing two villages with the slightly suggestive names of Pusselawa and Purpurasse, the steep climb up the Ramboda pass begins. This beautiful stretch of the road is lined with palmyras and rubber trees broken by long white bungalows, often wrapped in bougainvillea. Superb views can be obtained at intervals, while nearby winding waterfalls, luxuriant with ferns, embellish the harsh face of the mountain. Long before the summit of the pass is reached the atmosphere changes rapidly, and thick mists of the Scottish variety often make progress along this road both perilous and cold; the cautious traveller will therefore have warm clothes at hand. The change in temperature from Kandy, with its tropical heat, to Ramboda, which enjoys such a boreal climate, is most astonishing since the distance between them is only

Ceylon

thirty-three miles. From the heights the plains of Nuwara Eliya extend below, and the road runs down into the town, passing on the right Queen's Cottage, the residence of the Governor.

The second route from Kandy to Nuwara Eliya is a distance of seventy-three miles, and if Maskeliya is visited with the object of seeing or, in rarer cases, of climbing Adam's Peak, it is necessary from Hatton to make a detour of a further twelve miles. The same road, as on the first route, is taken to Gampola, and another eleven miles brings the traveller to Nawalapitiya, which boasts a railway and an "hotel." This is a famous district for tea plantations, although tea-bushes are small ornament to the countryside. After twenty-one miles through similar scenery Hatton is reached, whence a further twelve miles, south-east off the main road to Nuwara Eliya, lead to Maskeliya. This is a most delightful mountain road, edged with high ferns and bright cannas. Those staying at the excellent hotel at Hatton may be able to arrange to climb Adam's Peak.

It is usual to undertake this expedition between January and March, since the pilgrims during that time are a source of added interest to the traveller, and guides and coolies are easier to obtain. The approach to the peak from Maskeliya is now the

Pleasant Journeys

only one used, although great chains hanging on the south-western face of the mountain indicate that in the past the pilgrims attempted a more hazardous ascent. The chains were mentioned by Marco Polo in the thirteenth century, and tradition says they were placed there by Alexander the Great. Although, in fact, the approach from Maskeliya to the summit of the mountain is not dangerous climbing, the traveller should realize that Adam's Peak is seven thousand three hundred and fifty-three feet high, and it can only be reached after an arduous climb and a night spent in the open. Chills, and worse, can easily be caught in the ascent owing to heat, fatigue and rapid change of atmosphere, while to attempt to scale the peak during the rains is to court disaster. Having said this, the reader may not be surprised to learn that I admired the view and pondered on the significance of Adam's Peak from the comparative comfort of Maskeliya.

Adam's Peak is certainly the most famous mountain in Ceylon, resembling in shape a Brobdingnagian cone and dominating the landscape with an austere and even sinister ease. For the enterprising traveller on its summit at dawn, the peak's great shadow produces an awe-inspiring and even magical effect. The apex of the cone stretching

Ceylon

across jungle, tanks, palms and sea touches the distant horizon. Then as the sun rises the shadow slowly diminishes, until it vanishes at the foot of the mountain.

The concourse of pilgrims, which throng the mountain during the first three months of the year, is actuated by devotion towards the Sacred Footprint on the summit. This is encased in an open shrine and covered by a tiled roof. The Buddhists believe the print to be that of Buddha Gautama when, presumably to show his gymnastic prowess, he stood with one foot on Adam's Peak and the other on the ground, now enshrined by the Ruanweli Dagoba, one hundred and thirty miles away. The Hindus maintain that the footprint is that of the goddess Siva, while the Muhammadans venerate it as that of Adam, a belief which accounts for the mountain's name to-day. In the Koran it is written that after Adam's expulsion from Eden he was compelled to spend some years on a mountain in India before being permitted to rejoin his guilty spouse on Mount Arafath, near Mecca. Muhammadan seamen on their first arrival in Ceylon decided, for some obscure reason, that the summit of the peak had been Adam's place of atonement, and to-day both Shiyas and Sunnis reverence it as the "Hill of Our Father Adam."

Pleasant Journeys

A further element of competition arose when Christianity was introduced into the island, and the Portuguese announced that the Sacred Footprint had been made by St. Thomas the Apostle, who had been martyred near Madras in the year 75. Unfortunately, even Christian opinion was divided on the subject, since some maintained that the print was that of a nameless eunuch who had attended to the wants of Queen Caudace of Ethiopia, while Moses of Chorene in the fifth century bluntly stated that the footprint had been made by the Devil. As it is six feet long and nearly as wide across, this verdict appears in retrospect to be as good as any other.

Adam's Peak has contending names amongst the various sectaries, but there is one which rises in proud elegance above controversy: "Samanala Kanda," or the "Butterfly Rock." The peak earned this poetical appellation through the age-long incidence that, just before the monsoon, clouds of glorious butterflies float across Ceylon, as if seeking the refuge of Adam's Peak. Those who live near Ratnapura will also tell the traveller that the trees, which he might suppose had been bent nearly double by the south-west monsoon, are in fact performing a constant obeisance to the Sacred Footprint of the Lord Buddha.

Ceylon

Leaving the seclusion of Maskeliya and returning to the main road at Hatton, a further thirty miles through mountainous country will bring the visitor to the famous hill-station of Nuwara Eliya, which is six thousand two hundred and forty feet above sea-level. Much has been written about the "sporting" delights of this town, which can be enjoyed to the heart's content with a background of good hotels and "country clubs." The traveller requires no guide-book to these hedonistic pursuits, but rather some letters of introduction, which will give him the *entrée* to the homes and activities of the robust and hospitable inhabitants of Nuwara Eliya.

Two subjects, however, will probably interest the intelligent visitor: the rubber and tea plantations for which the neighbourhood is famous. The higher hills are used for tea, which can be grown up to an altitude of six thousand feet, while rubber cannot normally be grown over four thousand. The latter graceful trees belong almost entirely to the "Hevea" variety and cover nearly half a million acres of the island. When the bark is cut the rubber in the form of latex, or milk, flows into the little cups on the trees. The contents are collected into milk-pails and coagulated by acid. The rubber then undergoes different processes of washing and drying, according as to whether it is

Pleasant Journeys

to be sold in sheet or crepe form. A drying-room in a rubber factory is most attractive, as it appears to be festooned with immense curtains of Brussels lace. The planting of rubber trees in the island only dates from the 1890's, and the seeds were imported from Brazil. Large fortunes were made during the first ten years of this century, but the post-war years have not been so happy for the rubber planters in Ceylon.

Despite the hideous appearance of a tea-bush, these plantations seemed to me more interesting than those of rubber, perhaps from reasons of greed. Tea was introduced from China over fifty years ago, after the collapse of the coffee industry about 1880. The tea-plant belies its scrubby appearance by belonging to the camellia tribe, and in its wild state would grow to a height of thirty feet or more. But for practical reasons this is not allowed, and the tree is pruned to a height of two or three feet and encouraged to spread, in order to provide a better plucking surface. The poor bush is also not permitted to flower, since that denotes a lack of manure and consequent absence of adequate fertility. Tea-bushes grow on the slopes in plump serried rows, only relieved by an occasional and graceful acacia or grevillea, which acts as a "shade" tree.

Ceylon

The busiest months for plucking are from March to June, and in a lesser degree October and November, and it is delightful to watch the gaily dressed women nimbly throwing the leaves over their shoulders into the baskets on their backs. These pluckers put all their savings into gold ornaments, with which their bodies are plentifully adorned, and they belong exclusively to the Tamil race, since Singalese ladies decline to work in the rain. The women are paid by the pound of leaf, and during the most productive months one plucker can gather as much as seven pounds a day. The leaf is collected and weighed three times a day before being sent down to the factory. The average yield per acre is eight hundred pounds of tea, and the value of an acre in the market is approximately £150.

The average tea factory is a disconcerting if inevitable eyesore in this fine country. Here the leaf goes through a fourfold process in the most hygienic surroundings. It is first left to wither for twenty-four hours on jute shelves, then put through rollers when fermentation begins, and the green leaf assumes the colour of copper. "Firing" follows on perforated trays over which hot air is circulated by a fan, and after twenty minutes the tea emerges in its finished black and brittle form.

Pleasant Journeys

Sifting in automatic machines is the last process, which divides the leaves into seven different grades. The visitor to the factory will notice the ubiquitous "bloom" from the tea, which covers the structure with a furry substance, most irritating to the mucous membrane.

Much progress has been made in recent years towards improvement in the teaworkers' conditions of life. The "lines" which they inhabit must reach a reasonable hygienic standard, and on every estate there is a school supported, as to three-quarters of the total expenses, by the owner. A Hindu temple is often a decorative feature of a plantation, with an occasional chapel for the spiritual needs of the many Catholic Tamils. Although fuel and medical attendance are provided free, it is to be regretted that no old age pension scheme is in existence. The fact that few teaworkers live beyond their fifties seems an argument in favour of this humane measure, rather than the reverse.

The blame for such administrative shortcomings as may exist cannot in any way be attached to the planters on the estates, who only in rare instances are the actual owners. The latter are usually private or public companies operating in London and elsewhere, which therefore may be more interested

Ceylon

in their dividends than in the social conditions of those who help to make them. Nor, for the same reason, are the planters themselves responsible for the calamitous erosion of soil, which was the result of the widespread destruction of the high jungle in the past, in order to make room for tea. Thousands of acres of virgin forest were thus eliminated, and the clearings resulted in siltings and great floods owing to the top-soil being washed away by the rains. This deforestation, which in the low-country cost many lives, is now prohibited by Government, and to-day no new tracts of forest can be acquired for tea-planting in order to avoid further erosion, as well as the selfish destruction of the virgin jungle.

The road from Nuwara Eliya to Badulla, a distance of twenty-eight miles, passes through some of the most dramatic scenery in Ceylon. In this comparatively short distance the road drops from an altitude of over six thousand feet to one of two thousand, providing the traveller with an astonishing quick change of landscape. After leaving Hakgalla Pass, seven miles from Nuwara Eliya, where the Botanical Gardens should be seen, the road falls steeply, and from the mild climate and the lush vegetation of the "up-country" the traveller is suddenly precipitated into the dusty and torrid

Pleasant Journeys

zone of the *patanas*, which correspond to the English downland and are covered with coarse grass. This scenery is said to have reminded the Boer prisoners of war of the South African veldt. Wellimada, eleven miles from the Hakgalla gardens, is the first village reached. Although undistinguished, it possesses a pleasant rest-house, and the vicinity is known as "Little England." I was given two explanations of this unexpected appellation: firstly, because it resembles England—which it does not in any way, as far as my experience goes; and secondly, since it is, or was, partially inhabited by the past mistakes of the neighbouring Englishmen. Of the truth of this second explanation it was impossible to form any opinion.

Between Wellimada and Dikwella, a distance of six miles, the road undulates sharply; now down to the feet of overhanging mountains, then up to the heights of Etampitiya on an arid plateau, where a magnificent view back towards Nuwara Eliya can be obtained. The road from Dikwella to Badulla, a distance of four miles, skirting a deep valley covered with rubber, is shaded by an avenue of ingasaman trees. Badulla, the capital of the province of Uva, is famous for the beauty of the surrounding views, the charm of the river which encircles it, and the planters' club, where lavish

Ceylon

hospitality and a large variety of ball games can be enjoyed. I was assured that the members of this club are known as the "Merrie Men of Uva." In this town I discovered an object of melancholy interest in a neglected churchyard. Here is the tomb of one Sophia Wilson, a wife of a former Agent of the district. It is to-day in the tenacious grip of an ancient and sinister Bo-tree. The tomb is dated 1817.

The distance from Badulla to Haputale is twenty-five miles, and the traveller must retrace his steps to Dikwella and then take the left-hand road to Bandarawela, eighteen miles away. Thence there is a climb of about two thousand feet through a parched or green valley, according to the time of the year. Bandarawela possesses an hotel, a railway station and a club, while nearby lies the hill-station of Diyatalawa, which may provide a thrill for the naval-minded visitor. Here officers and men of the Royal Navy enjoy an occasional respite from the tropical heat of Colombo and Trincomalee. It was originally a camp for the luckless Boer prisoners of war. After a further seven miles and a climb of six hundred feet Haputale is reached, where the traveller will experience the sensation of being on the top of the world. There is an excellent rest-house here, and the views are unrivalled in

Pleasant Journeys

Ceylon. On a fine day the sea beyond Hambantota is visible, while to the north-east the Haputale range stretches back to Badulla. Unfortunately I arrived at Haputale in a thick wet mist, and the straggling town under that condition reminded me irresistibly of one of the bleaker villages in the Scottish Highlands. But the great packs of clouds in the valley below served to emphasize its altitude and isolation.

From Haputale to Haldumulla is a distance of seven miles with a descent of one thousand three hundred feet. It is a steep and winding road with fine views of the low-country stretching to Hambantota. The small rest-house at Haldumulla, apart from providing excellent food, is as well situated as any in the interior of the island. I shall never forget sitting on the verandah there and watching the grey mist below being dissipated by the sun, until the distant green mountains of Kataragama emerged like a line of mammoth elephants, urged by a mutual desire to descend to the sea.

The road from Haldumulla to Balangoda, a distance of twenty-two miles with a descent of over three thousand feet, lies through a rich and varied landscape, mingling up-country with jungle scenery until rubber, tea and coconut plantations are reached in the plain. Between Balangoda and Rat-

Ceylon

napura, a distance of twenty-seven miles, lies some of the best rubber country in Ceylon. It is a pretty and undulating road, with emerald-green paddy-fields on either side, stretching away to the distant hills.

Ratnapura, provided with a good rest-house, is in the heart of the rubber country, but its excessively hot and moist climate makes a prolonged stay disagreeable for the traveller. There is, however, one compensation, since in this humid temperature all vegetation seems to be more lush and luxurious than elsewhere. Greens are more vivid, yellows more harsh and bright, while the red hibiscus appears to grow to double its normal size. Ratnapura, besides being a rubber centre, is famous for its gem industry, which has provided both East and West with the largest and most beautiful stones since the earliest times. These jewels are found in the gravel deposits in the beds of the neighbouring rivers. The gravel is forced through wide-meshed sieves, and then the gems either do, or do not, emerge. Although the "gemmers" are usually Singalese, the cutters and polishers are always Moors.

The most lovely jewel to be found in Ceylon is the star-sapphire. This varies from a pale grey to a vivid dark blue, with the star formation in the

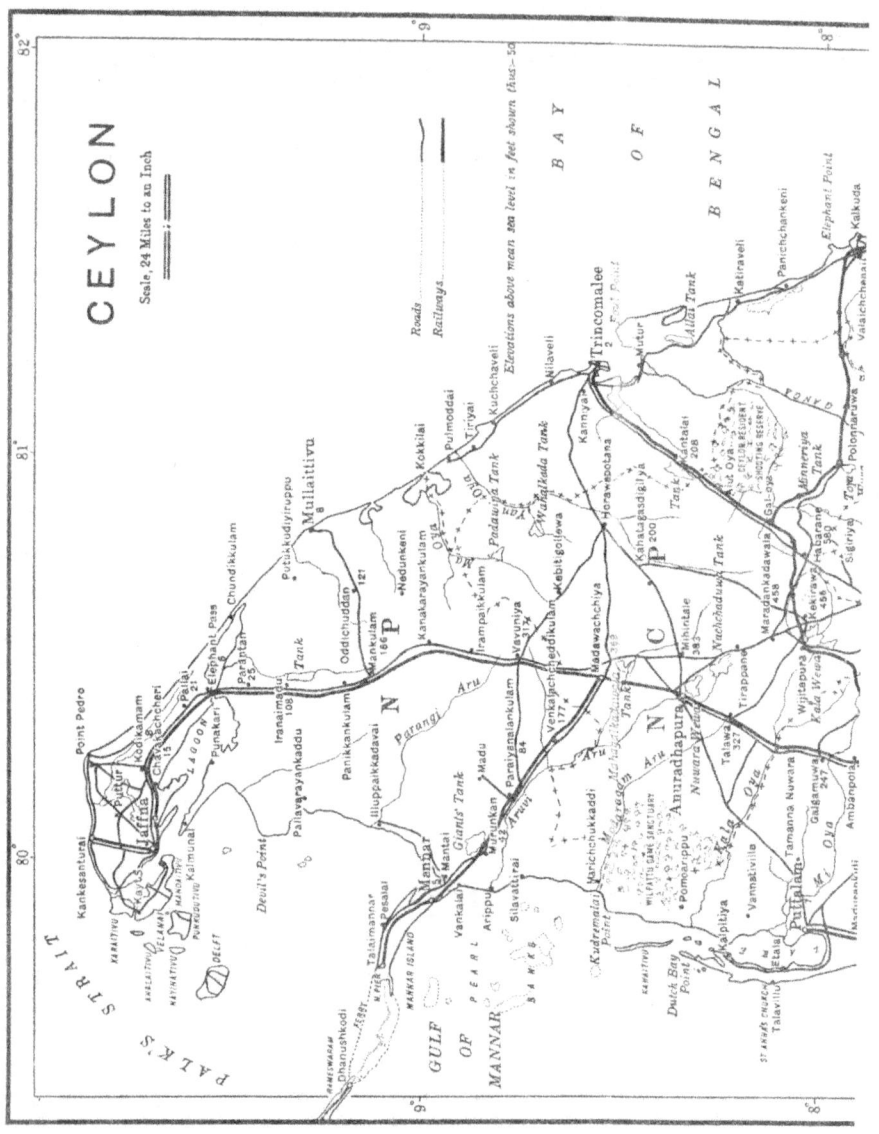

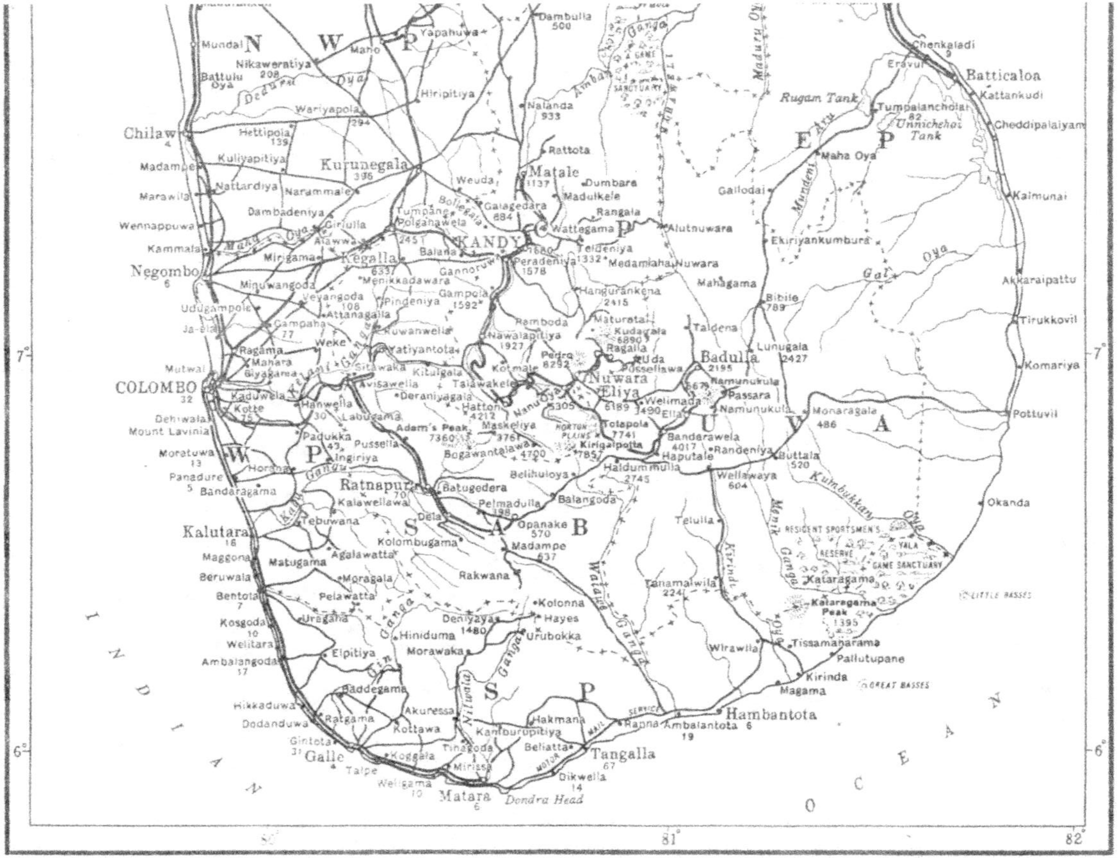

For use in book "CEYLON," published by George Allen & Unwin Ltd., London

Pleasant Journeys

centre. The Hindus have a delightful legend that if this gem is worn on the left hand, it will guard the wearer against evil, since the star is symbolic of captive fire, long worshipped by them as a sure protection against evil. Amongst other stones found near Ratnapura are aquamarines, rubies, amethysts, tourmalines, alexandrites, zircons, chrysoberyls and spinels. Garnets and moonstones are the cheapest to buy, while the curious "catseye," with a streak of light across the centre of the gem, is to-day of comparative little value. In the seventeenth century, however, this rather ugly stone to modern eyes was highly prized, since the Portuguese traveller Ribeiro wrote at that period: "The most precious stones in the island of Ceylon, amongst both the Moors and Gentiles, are the catseyes. One hardly ever sees them in Europe. I once saw one, as big as a pigeon's egg, on the arm of the Prince of Uva. . . . This stone was entirely round and made like a large ball for an arquebus."

Leaving clammy Ratnapura, the traveller now takes the road to Colombo via Avisawella, a distance of fifty-six miles. The route passes through the pretty but populous Kelani valley, where planters of rubber abound. At Kuruwita, nine miles out of Ratnapura, a magnificent view of

Ceylon

Adam's Peak can be enjoyed. Here there is a pilgrims' path to the peak, but it is now little used owing to the arduous ascent on the western side. The twenty-nine-mile road from Avisawella to Colombo has already been described.

In completing the fifth and last of our "Pleasant Journeys," I must thank the traveller for his presumptive patience in my invisible company. He has also provided me with a happy pretext for revisiting, in the spirit, the beautiful island of Ceylon.

INDEX

Abhaya, tank, 70
Abhayagiriya Dagoba, 126, 127
Adam's Bridge, 41
Adam's Peak, 23, 29, 176, 268, 292, 293–4, 295, 306
Ajanta, 151
Ajohhya, Sagara, King of, 174
Alexander the Great, 293
Alms-hall, 113
Aluvihare, 175–176, 268
Ambalangoda, 223, 224
Ambasthala Dagoba, 114
Ambepussa, 279
Ananda, 142
Andrews, (—), 102
Animals, 37, 38, 39, 40, 41, 42, 44, 47, 48, 180 et seq., 193 et seq., 243
Ants, 181–182, 261, 262
Anula, Queen, 80, 81
Anuradha, 70
Anuradhapura, 13, 26, 27, 28, 69, 70, 71, 73, 74, 75, 77, 78, 79, 80, 82, 83, 85, 86, 111, 112, 113, 115, 116–134, 136, 139, 141, 145, 149, 159, 161, 162, 168, 171, 172, 255, 256, 263, 265, 282, 288
Anuradhapura-Jaffna road, 245
Archaeological Commissioner and Survey, 112, 117, 119, 143, 145, 173, 174
Arnold, Edwin, 166
Arrack, 248
Arugam Bay, 188, 232, 233, 237, 263
Arugam Tank, 232

Asoka, 71, 108
Audience Hall, 150
Aukana Vihara, 177–179, 265
Avisawella, 277, 278, 305, 306
Ayikas, 108

Badulla, 300, 301, 302, 303
Balakaduwa Pass, 268
Balangoda, 303
Bambalapitiya, 215
Bandaranaike, Sir Solomon, 279
Bandarawela, 302
Barnes, Sir Edward, 221, 270
Bat Drive, 273, 274
Batticaloa, 224, 226, 233, 234, 235, 236, 237, 239, 240, 283
Battulu-oya, 286
Bees, swarms of, 154, 155
Bell, (—), 143
Benares, Deer Park at, 55, 58
Bengal: King of, 164; kingdom of, 65
Bentota, 223, 224
Bhatikabhaya, 81, 82
Bhikkhus, 54, 59, 60, 61, 62, 79, 82, 106, 107, 114, 117, 120, 121, 125, 129, 149, 159, 161, 162, 163, 165, 166, 168, 172, 175, 176, 178
Bhuvaneka Bahu I, King, 92, 145, 146
Bible Rock, 278, 279
Bihar, Princedom of, 55
Birds, 187, 188, 189, 206–209, 258, 259
Black rock Vihara, 142
Blake, Lady, 270, 271

307

Ceylon

Bodhi, *see* Bo-tree
Botanic Gardens, Royal, 271, 272, 273, 278
Botanical Gardens, 300
Bo-tree (Bodhi), 55, 72, 73, 117, 118, 120, 121, 161, 165, 178, 302
Bottuwa plains, 185, 186
Brazen Palace, 82, 111, 118, 119
Buddha, 13, 52–63, 89, 108, 110, 111, 119, 123, 131, 132, 135, 137, 138, 139, 140, 141, 142, 143, 144, 160, 161, 162, 165, 168, 170, 171, 172, 175, 177, 178, 179, 253, 274, 294
Buddha, Dhamma, and Samgha, 58, 60, 63, 128
Buddhadaasa, King, 84
Buddhism and Buddhists, 17, 18, 22, 23, 26, 52, 71, 73, 86, 93, 94, 107, 108, 111, 117, 122, 160, 163, 167, 169, 179, 294
Buddhist calendar, 61
Buddhist Shrines and Temples, 124, 160–179
Bullock Street, 133
Burghers, 17, 18, 21
Buttala, 231
Butterflies, 261, 295
Butterfly Rock, 295

Calvinism, 95
Catharina, Donna, 93, 94
Caudace, Queen, of Ethiopia, 295
Ceilao, 15
Cetiya of Ruanweli, 81
Channa, charioteer, 54

Chilaw, 256, 285, 286
Chilaw-Puttalam road, 287
Chilli Dagoba, 124, 125
China, and Chinese, 89, 90, 101, 297
Ching-Ho, General, 89
Cholas, 135, 144, 177, *see also* Tamils
Cinnamon Gardens, 215, 220
Climate, 24, 25, 26
Clothes, significance of, 18, 19, 20, 21
Cobra Rock, 150
Colombo, 27, 90, 92, 93, 94, 99, 100, 104, 106, 200, 214–223, 302
Colombo Museum, 163
Colpetty, 215
Connaught, Duke and Duchess of, 154
Coranga, 80, 81
Cotta, 88, 90, 91, 93, 147, 162
Cottiar, fort at, 94

Dagobas, 13, 87, 107–109, 160, 168
Dalada Maligawa, or Tooth Temple, *see* Tooth Temple
Dambulla, rock temple at, 106, 169–172, 175, 263, 267
Daulagalla, 274, 275
Degaldoruwa, 168, 169
Demala-Maha-Seya, 143, 144
Detutissa, King, 84
Devadatta, 55
Devanampiyatissa, 70, 71, 72, 73, 74, 75, 108, 110
Devil-dancing, 23, 24
Dewa Raja Vihara, 170

Index

Dharmapala Bahu, King Don Juan, 92, 93
Dhatu Sena, King, 84, 148, 149, 178
Dikwella, 301, 302
Diyatalawa, 302
Dondra Head, 227
Dumbara Valley, 271
Dutch, the, 15, 16, 17, 21, 91, 94, 95, 96, 99, 100, 101, 214, 217, 218, 223, 225, 235, 250, 251, 252, 283, 284, 287
Dutch East India Company, 168
Dutch Point Bay, 287
Dutthagamani, 76, 77, 78, 79, 118, 119, 120, 121, 122, 124, 125, 131, 132, 158, 171

East India Company: British, 102; Dutch, 168; United, 225
Eight Sacred Places, 116, 123, 126, 127
Elara, 74, 75, 76, 77, 78, 79, 171
Elephant Pass, 246
Elephant Pokuna, 130
Elephant Rock, 277
Elephant stables, 129, 130
Elephants, 105
Elizabeth, Queen, 101
Etalai tank, 286, 287
Etampitiya, 301
Eurasians, 17, 21

Fa-Hien, 13, 89
Fitch, Ralph, 101
Flower-stem Hall, 138
Flowers, 189 et seq., 272–273

Footprint, Sacred, 294, 295
Forest Conservancy, 200
Fort Frederick, 241
Francis Xavier, St., 93

Gadaladeniya temple, 271, 274, 275
Gal, 142, 143
Galagedava Pass, 277
Galgammuwa, 288, 289
Galgammuwa tank, 200, 288
Galle, 28, 101, 214, 215, 218, 225, 226
Galle-Face Esplanade, 218
Galpota, 140
Gal-Vihara images, 178
Gamani, 76
Gampola, 275, 277, 291, 292
Gaspar Peria-Perumal, 253
Gautama, Buddha, *see* Buddha
Gaya, Buddha, 73
Gedi-Gé, 176–177, 267
Geiger, Prof. W., 52
Gem Pavilion, 118, 119
Gems, 304–305
Giant's tank, 200
Gin-Ganga, 223
Ginigathena Gap, 277
Giriulla, 277
Goa, 95, 162
Golden-spire Monastery, 140
Gordon, Lady, 271
Gourds, village of the, 69
Great King Street, 133
Great New Temple, 171
Great Temple, 117
Guardstone, 129, 141
Guilford, Hon. F. North, Lord, 103, 104

Ceylon

Habarane, 260, 261, 263
Hakgalla Gardens, 301
Hakgalla Pass, 300
Haldumulla, 303
Halloluwa Road, 271
Hambantota, 226, 228, 229, 256, 303
Hansa, 128
Hanwella, 278
Haputale, 302, 303
Hata-dagé, 140
Hatton, 291, 292, 296
Heber, Mrs., 14, 15, 269
Hikkaduwa, 225
Himalayas, 88
Hinduism, 161
Hindus, the, 17, 18, 22, 23, 86, 253
Holland, 102, 217, 226
Horawapotana, 244, 256, 257
Horton, Lady, 270
Horton, Sir R. W., 217

Insects, 34, 35, 36, 38, 46, 181
Isurumuniya, 125, 172–175

Jaffna, 20, 246, 247, 248, 249, 250, 253, 254, 256, 283
Ja-ela, 282
Jatakas, 144
Jathale Dagoba, 110
Jaya-Weira, 92, 93
Jetawanarama Dagoba, 83, 126, 127, 130, 131
Jewel of Ceylon Temple, 141
John III of Portugal, 92
Juan (Prince Dharmapala), 92
Jungle, the, 28, 29, 49, 125, 136, 180–209, 243

Kadugannawa, 274, 275, 278
Kakavannatissa, King, 75, 76
Kala-oya, 288
Kalawewa, 178, 179, 263, 265
Kalidassa, 84
Kalkuda Bay, 226, 237, 238, 239, 263
Kalmunai, 233, 234
Kalpitiya, 286, 287
Kalutara, 192, 222, 223
Kandula, 77, 78, 124, 158
Kanduwela, 278
Kandy, 27, 88, 93, 100, 103, 104, 105, 106, 147, 161, 163, 167, 168, 261, 266, 268, 270, 271, 278, 290, 291
Kandyan regalia, 269
Kankesanturai, 253
Kanniyai, 244
Kannya, 244
Kantaka Cetiya Dagoba, 112, 113
Kantalai, 257, 258, 259, 260
Kantalai, great tanks at, 83
Kanthaka, 54, 77
Kanthriyagama tank, 266
Kapilavastu, 52, 54, 141
Kasyapa, 85, 148, 149, 150, 151, 152, 153, 155, 156, 157, 158
Kataragama, 229, 303
Katiraveli, 239
Kegalla, 277, 278, 279
Kekirawa, 184, 200, 237, 256, 263, 264, 265, 266, 282, 288, 289
Kelani, 278, 305
Kelani River, 278
King's Palace, 127, 128, 129
King's Pavilion, 168
Kiri, or Milk-White Dagoba, 142

Index

Knox, Robert, 14, 20, 22, 96, 97, 98, 99, 100, 102, 182, 187, 190, 274
Koddiyar, 239
Konde, the, 19
Kuda Akibo, King, 85
Kumavadasen, King, 84
Kurumba, 114
Kurunegala, 276, 277
Kuruwita, 305
Kusinava, 57
Kutakannatissa, 81
Kuttam Pokuna, 130

Lanjatissa, King, 113
Lanka, 16, 56, 73, 76, 77, 78, 80, 82, 84, 85, 87, 88, 91, 101, 106, 134, 143, 145, 146, 149, 157, 158, 161, 162, 175
Lankarama Dagoba, 127
Lankatilaka (Jewel of Ceylon) Temple, 141, 144, 177, 271, 274, 275
Latamandapa, or Flower-stem Hall, 138
Leelavati, Queen, 87
Lewella ferry, 168
Lion Rock, *see* Sigiriya
Lion Throne, 151
Loadstone Mountain, 222
Lohapasada, or Brazen Palace, 82, 111, 118, 119, 121
Longden, Lady, 270, 271
Lost Cities, 27, 29, 52, 107–147

McCarthy, Lady, 271
McDowell, Gen., 104
Madawachchiya, 254, 255
Madhu, 287, 288

Magama, 109
Maha Alut Vihara, 171
Mahabalipuram, 151
Mahadathikamahanaga, 112
Maha Dewala, 168
Maha-meru-gala, 150
Mahasaya Dagoba, 115
Mahasena, King, 82, 83, 257, 260
Mahavihara, or Great Temple, 117
Mahawamsa, the, 52, 56, 57, 64–83, 96, 114, 116, 118, 119, 120, 121
Mahaweliganga, 271, 273
Mahaweliganga River, 68, 278
Mahinda, 71, 72, 111, 115
Mahinda's bed, 115
Maho road, 286
Maitreya, 60
Makaras, 113, 139
Malabar, 101
Malabar Street, 271
Malayans, 20
Malwatta Temple, 168
Mandapaya Vihara, 142
Manik Dagoba, 110
Mankulam, 245, 246
Mankulam-Jaffna road, 246
Mannar, 254, 255
Mantharams, 202, 203
Mara (Satan), 55
Maskeliya, 291, 292, 293, 296
Matale, 149, 175, 267, 268
Matara, 200, 226, 227
Mawanella, 278
Maya, Queen, 52, 53
Migara, 148, 149
Mihintale, 29, 71, 72, 111–116, 140, 182, 256
Milk-white Dagoba, 142
Mineriya, great tanks at, 83, 260

Ceylon

Mirisawetiya Dagoba, 124, 125, 129
Mogallana, 148, 149, 157, 158
Monargalla, 231, 232
Monsoons, 25
Moonstone, 127, 128
Moon Street, 133
Moors, the, 17, 18, 102, 287
Moses of Chorene, 295
Mount Arafath, 294
Mount Lavinia, 221, 222, 223, 271
Muhammadans, 18
Mullaittivu, 246, 254
Mundel, 286
Munessaram, 286
Munro, Sir Hector, 102
Museum, The, 274
Mutur, 239

Naga, 121, 129, 139
Naga Pokuna, or Snake's bathing pool, 115
Nalagiri, 55
Nalanda, 176, 267
Nanu-oya, 275
Nata Dewala, 167, 168
Nawalapitiya, 291, 292
Negombo, 256, 276, 277, 282, 283, 284, 285
Nil-Ganga (Blue River), 200, 227
Niliya, 81
Nirvana, 57, 58, 59, 60, 61, 62, 142, 143
Nissanka, Malla, King, 138, 140, 141, 144
North, Hon. F., see Guilford
Nuwara Eliya, 25, 28, 291, 292, 296, 300, 301

Old Palace, 268, 269
Orawela, forests of, 54

Paddy, cultivation of, 279-280
Palai, 248
Pali, Princess, 67, 68
Palk Bay, 255
Pallavan, artists, 173, 175
Pandukabhaya, 66, 67, 68, 69, 70, 77
Panduvasudeva, 66
Pandy, King of, 86
Panichchankeni, 239
Parakrama Bahu I, King, 85, 86, 87, 88, 135, 136, 137, 141, 142, 162, 175
Parakrama Bahu III, 162
Parakrama Bahu, VI, King, 89, 90
Parantan, 246
Parati, 173
Parsees, 102
Peacock Palace, 118
Pearl Dagoba, 110
Pekin, Singalese mission to, 89
Peradeniya gardens, 189-190
Peradeniya Road, 271, 274, 277
Perahera festival, 163, 167
Piduragala Vihara at, 152
Pitt, W., 103
Point Pedro, 253
Pokuna, 114, 130
Polo, Marco, 14, 293
Polonnaruwa, 26, 28, 85, 86, 88, 116, 134-145, 162, 177, 178, 260, 261, 263
Portuguese, 15, 16, 17, 21, 90, 91, 92, 93, 94, 95, 96, 99, 100, 101, 146, 162, 214, 234, 241, 250, 283, 284, 287, 295

Index

Poson, 167
Potgul Vehera, 136
Pottuvil, 226, 231, 232, 233, 234
Poya-gé, 168
Priests, *see* Bhikkhus
Purpurasse, 291
Pusselawa, 291
Puttalam, 66, 199, 200, 286, 287, 288

Queen's Cottage, 292
Queen's Pavilion, 130

Races and Religions, 17–18
Rahula, 53
Rajaviliya, 64, 70, 83, 84, 88, 90, 93
Rama, 41
Ramayana, 174
Ramboda Pass, 291
Rankot Vehera, 140, 141, 142
Ratnapura, 295, 303–304, 305
Ravana, King, 244
Reder, Admiral, 252
Ribeiro, 305
River Drive, 273
River Street, 133
Rodiya, 275, 276
Rohuna, 75, 76, 85
Roman Catholics, 18, 91, 92, 94, 95, 100, 284–285, 286
Royal Botanic Gardens, 271–273, 278
Royal Palace, 145
Ruanweli, Great Cetiya of, 81, 82, 119, 120, 121, 122, 123, 133, 168, 294
Rupavati, 136
Rupavati, Queen, 87

Sacred Mountain, 111, 113, 116
Sagara, King of Ajohhya, 174
Sage Kapila, 174
Sahri, 20, 21
St. Thomas, 295
Samanala Kanda, or the Butterfly Rock, 295
Samgha, 60
Sardiel, 279
Sarong, the, 18, 19, 21
Sat-Mahal-Prasada, 139
Sena, King Maha, 126
Senarat, King, 93, 94
Serendib, 15
Siddhartha Gautama, 52, 53, 54
Sigiriya, or the Lion Rock, 28, 85, 116, 148–159, 169, 189, 261, 262, 263, 264
Sihabahu, 65
Sihagiri, 149
Singalese, 16, 17, 18, 19, 20, 22, 23, 52
Sinha, Narenda, King, 164
Sinha, King Raja, 20, 92, 93
Sinha, Rajadi Raja, King, 269
Sinha II, Raja, 94, 96, 97, 98, 99, 100, 101
Sinha, Sri Wikrema Raja, King, 103, 104, 105, 164, 270
Sinhala Dvipa, 15
Siva, 80, 173, 241, 294
Siva Devale, 137, 138
Snake's bathing pool, 115
Sopater, 13
Sri, goddess of fortune, 140
Still, John, 201
Stone Book, 140
Stone canoes, 130, 131
Suddhodana of the Sakyas, 52, 54
Sulawamsa, the, 83–106

Ceylon

Sumati, Queen, 174
Sunnis, 294
Superstitions, 22, 23, 24
Swami Rock, 241

Talawa, 265, 266, 288, 289
Talawewa, 289
Talipot Avenue, 273
Tamils, the, 16, 17, 18, 19, 20, 22, 23, 26, 77, 78, 80, 83, 84, 85, 86, 88, 101, 132, 141, 145, 146, 148, 177, 234, 241, 245, 249, 250, see also Cholas
Tangalla, 226, 228
Taprobane, 15
Tea plantations, 296–300
Temples, Buddhist, 160–179
Tennant, Sir James, 126, 254, 260, 276
Thera, 115
Thupa, the Great, 80, 82
Thuparama Dagoba, 73, 123, 124, 126, 127, 138, 141, 144, 177
Tirappane, 288
Tissa, 76, 79, 80, 81, 113, 114, 131, 172
Tissa, Queen, 111
Tissamaharama, 109–111, 147, 199, 200, 229, 230
Tissamaharama Dagoba, 110
Tissawewa, 125, 172

Tooth Temple (Dalada Maligawa), 124, 137, 140, 145, 161, 163, 164, 165, 166, 167, 168, 169, 268, 269, 270
Topawewa tank, 260
Torrington, Lord, 106
Trees, 191–193

Trincomalee, 14, 27, 94, 96, 102, 111, 195, 226, 236, 239, 240, 241, 256, 257, 267, 278, 282, 302
Trincomalee Street, 271
Twin Baths, 130

Udugalpitiya, 271, 275, 276
United East India Company, 225
Upatissa, King, 260
Upper Lake Road, 270
Uva, 301, 305

Vakaneri tank, 238
Valaichchenai, 237, 239
Van Eck, Governor, 227
Van Rhede, Francina, 241
Vanni, 245
Varuna, 129
Vatthagamani, 80
Vatuka, 80
Vavuniya, 200, 244, 245
Veddahs, 236
Vedikas, 108
Vergonce, Father, 100
Veti, 19
Veyangoda, 277, 278, 279, 280, 281
Viharadevi, 75, 76
Viharas, 113, 118, 126, 127, 130, 152, 175, 177, 178, 179
Vijaya I, 64, 66, 82, 85, 255
Vijaya Bahu IV, 89
Vishnu, 161, 170, 244

Wace Park, 270
Walagambahu, King, 169, 171, 175

Index

Wata-dagé, 138, 139
Wellawaya, 231, 256
Wellimada, 301
Wesak, 61, 167
Wijabahu I, King, 135
Wijabahu IV, King, 141
Wijito, 77, 78
Wikramabahu, King, 162, 163
Wilson, Sophia, 302
Wimala Dhamma, 93, 94
Wimala Dhamma Suriya II, King, 164

Wirawila, 229, 230
Wolfenhal Church, 217

Yakkhas, 54, 56
Yakkhini, 68, 69, 70, 77
Yala game sanctuary, 111, 186, 199, 230
Yapahuwa, 88, 145–147, 162, 263, 288, 289
Yasodara, Princess, 52
Yatiyantota, 278

GEORGE ALLEN & UNWIN LTD
LONDON: 40 MUSEUM STREET, W.C.1
LEIPZIG: (F. VOLCKMAR) HOSPITALSTR. 10
CAPE TOWN: 73 ST. GEORGE'S STREET
TORONTO: 91 WELLINGTON STREET, WEST
BOMBAY: 15 GRAHAM ROAD, BALLARD ESTATE
WELLINGTON, N.Z.: 8 KINGS CRESCENT, LOWER HUTT
SYDNEY, N.S.W.: AUSTRALIA HOUSE, WYNYARD SQUARE

Travels in the North
by KAREL ČAPEK
Translated by M. *and* R. Weatherall
Illustrated. Cr. 8vo.   7s. 6d.

Čapek travelled north beyond the Arctic Circle because he wanted to see at last the lands of his boyish dreams, and of his life-long friends, Kierkegaard, Jacobsen, and the others, and also because the silvery and cool birch-trees, the aconites, the moss, and the sparkling waters appeal to him strongly. He tells of his impressions in the generous style of a smiling philosopher and there is great mellowness and depth in his observations.

Introducing Britain
by THOMAS BURKE, S. P. B. MAIS, *and others*
Illustrated. Cr. 8vo.   7s. 6d.

"A collection of impressions of British life and landscape, this book is an outstanding event in the production of travel literature . . . the book should serve not only as an introduction to Britain for the visitor, but also as a contribution to our own knowledge of our country. . . . Subjects have been cleverly selected, and photographs are of a high standard. . . . All that is best in English life and scenery is described, and the reader can obtain, by reading well-written essays, an impression and understanding of England such as no guide-book could offer . . . exceptionally satisfying travel book."—*Tourist*

A Tour in Northumbria
by DOUGLAS GOLDRING

8¾ × 6½ *in. wide; with* 28 *photographic illustrations.*   7s. 6d.

Many people hurry through Northumbria intent only on arriving somewhere else. Mr. Goldring, however, went there on a leisurely tour for no other reason than to see what it was like. He found busy cities, quaint market towns, hamlets, and fishing villages. The countryside varied between remote, lovely moorland, thickly wooded valleys, and sandy sea-coast. Castles, border fortresses, and old ecclesiastical buildings with their long romantic histories proved absorbingly interesting. All these things are described vividly and lucidly. Mr. Goldring has the experienced traveller's knack of picking out the essential characteristics of places seen.

This book about Northumbria is packed with local information and sensible advice on what and what not to see, where to go for the best sport, and where to stay. It also gives lightly and entertainingly a story of life as it is in the two most northerly counties of England to-day.

From My African Notebook
by Dr. ALBERT SCHWEITZER
Author of *My Life and Thought, Christianity and the Religions of the World*, etc.
Translated by Lilian Russell

Illustrated. Cr. 8vo. 5s.

In this little volume, written in the vein of his ever-popular *On the Edge of the Primeval Forest*, Dr. Schweitzer, from his unique wealth of experience, gives us a rich medley of history, reflection, folklore, marriage and birth customs, and stories. His keen sense of humour has made the book intensely amusing, but at the same time it adds much to our understanding of primitive mentality and should not be missed by anyone concerned with Africans. The chapter on Taboos and Magic is of special interest and helps us to realize in what a state of spiritual bondage pagan peoples may live. It will be news to many people that the hospital at Lambaréné occupies the site of Aloysius Horn's African home. A whole chapter is devoted to Trader Horn and his contemporaries. Altogether a most enlightening work, though light enough to be enjoyed even by intelligent children.

Language Hunting in the Karakoram
by E. O. LORIMER

Illustrated. Demy 8vo. 12s. 6d.

In an almost inaccessible part of the Karakoram, in the extreme north of British India, on the frontier of Afghanistan and Chinese Turkestan, lives an entirely self-supporting peasant people, the Burusho of Hunza. They have been ruled by their own royal family for at least six hundred years; they have no machines and almost no money, but their social organization is as admirable as their material culture is primitive. Mrs. Lorimer and her husband lived for a year amongst them and were the first white people to learn their difficult language, which is apparently unrelated to any other speech, alive or dead. Mrs. Lorimer tells of the delightful life amongst these people, of the beauty of the Karakoram and the adventurous journey through high mountains that she and her husband made to get there. There are many very beautiful photographs.

The Waters of the West
by KENNETH PRINGLE

Demy 8vo. 12s. 6d.

"For three and a half years Mr. Pringle was a schoolmaster in Jamaica. He made good use of his eyes and ears during that time. Now in a book that is brilliantly written he throws light on the causes of the discontent that led to recent disturbances."—*Reynolds News*

Maltese Memories
by Eric Brockman

Illustrated. Cr. 8vo. 6s.

To most Englishmen who have not had the necessity to live in Malta, the name conveys little more than a place of strategic importance, a fortified harbour and ships of war. To a lesser degree it is associated with the Knights of St. John. But relatively few know that Malta has a people all its own, with traditions and customs as unique as they are picturesque, or that it was not until after the Great War that the island took its first hesitant step into the twentieth century. Lt.-Commander Brockman has, in this volume, recorded briefly and colourfully the romantic history of the island from the time of the Phoenicians, and has much to tell too of the Maltese people, their life and laws and customs, their songs and festivals. Very little has been written of Malta and Lt.-Commander Brockman's book is badly wanted.

Sweden: Ancient and Modern
compiled and edited by Rolf Gruaers
Foreword by Vernon Bartlett

Demy 8vo. 5s.

This book, which is at once a concise history and a practical guide-book, aims at making Sweden better known to the English-speaking world. The conditions of present-day Sweden are shown against a background of centuries of development, and the lively and attractive style in which the book is written does not preclude the incorporation of a great deal of exact information which will help the reader to form a true and clear conception of the land and its people. The book is profusely illustrated and includes a number of maps and diagrams.

The Green Edge of Asia
by Richard Pyke

Illustrated. La. Cr. 8vo. 6s.

"What he saw he recorded with an artist's intuition. There can be few books so short that reward the reader so handsomely—and few books of travel, one feels, should be longer. In these sketches of things seen, felt, and heard, we get more genuine information, more intelligent appraisement, than in a library—full of conscientious wanderings. There is no padding in the little record, and few things that are not reported at first-hand."—*Sunday Times*

Down River

A CANOE TOUR ON THE SEVERN AND THE THAMES

by G. M. BOUMPHREY

Author of *Along the Roman Roads, The House Inside and Out*, etc.

Narrow Cr. 8vo.   4s. 6d.

G. M. Boumphrey's delightful book *Along the Roman Roads* will be remembered with pleasure by thousands of readers as well as by his countless listening public. *Down River* describes his adventures and impressions of a voyage down the Severn and Upper Thames in a portable canoe. The broadcasts on which the book is founded proved one of the most popular features of the Talks Programmes during the past summer. Here is an opportunity to recapture the enjoyment they gave.

The book contains a number of attractive photos by the author.

(George Allen & Unwin's Pocket Crowns, No. 12)

A Vagabond's Way

by NANCY PRICE

With numerous line-drawings and 17 half-tone illustrations.   Cr. 8vo.   5s.

Miss Nancy Price is well known for her work in connection with the People's National Theatre. She combines her wide knowledge of drama and the theatre with a deep love for the lakes, fells, and valleys of the north of England, and in *A Vagabond's Way* (now re-issued by this firm in a new and cheap edition) she writes of leisurely rambles in Westmorland and Cumberland, not as a tourist but as one who really knows the Lake Country in all its moods, and who understands and appreciates the people who live there.

Where Shall We Go This Year?

AN UNBIASED GUIDE TO EAST COAST RESORTS

by G. H. BOSWORTH

Illustrated.   Cr. 8vo.   2s. 6d.

Nearly all the existing guides to seaside resorts are issued by prejudiced parties. The railway companies and the local Town Councils and Chambers of Commerce can hardly be expected to take a purely objective view of the places on which their prosperity depends. This guide, in addition to giving a comprehensive account of the attractions and advantages of all the resorts on the East Coast, is perfectly frank about their unattractive sides and their disadvantages. Thousands who have been misled by optimistic "puffs" of So-and-So-on-Sea and have wasted a holiday in an unsuitable place will welcome this volume.

All prices are net

LONDON: GEORGE ALLEN & UNWIN LTD

For Product Safety Concerns and Information please contact our EU representative GPSR@taylorandfrancis.com
Taylor & Francis Verlag GmbH, Kaufingerstraße 24, 80331 München, Germany

www.ingramcontent.com/pod-product-compliance
Lightning Source LLC
Chambersburg PA
CBHW071758300426
44116CB00009B/1124